# Within These
# Four Walls

Cover Illustration and design: Evie Torrance

For all inquiries: evie@mindfullyevie.com

ISBN: 9781083191748

# Within These Four Walls

By Mindfully Evie

# Table of contents

# Introduction

Every word written in this book was written from within the confines of my home. Spanning over nearly three years this book is a testament to my time being housebound and proof that despite all the suffering, there is always happiness to be created, peace to be unearthed, and a life to be lived.

A journey of self-discovery and personal growth, I hope this book may offer you comfort, inspiration, and wisdom, whatever path you find yourself on. And I hope by sharing my story and imparting my thoughts, it may help you in some small way too.

## About me

The last time I left the house was 29th November 2016. You're probably wondering why, and while I could go into the details of the diagnosis, I'm going to keep it simple and say I suffer from severe Myalgic Encephalomyelitis (M.E) and Chronic Lyme disease. It's hard to articulate precisely what those chronic illnesses entail in general, as it is different for every single person. But for me, more than anything, it involves crushing and incurable fatigue.

# Introduction

My body does not produce enough energy. If you imagine your energy like a battery charge, each day a healthy person would start the day at 100% charge whereas I would start the day with 10–20%. This results in me barely having enough energy to get through the day. Other symptoms I suffer from as a result of M.E and Chronic Lyme, include pain, migraines, an inability to regulate body temperature, and severe noise and light sensitivity.

Despite only being twenty-two, despite not leaving the house for nearly three years, and despite not being well enough to see my friends and family, I can honestly say I have never been happier. These last few years of being completely housebound, and at the time of writing this, bedbound, have been the catalyst of a journey of personal discovery and growth, going beyond depths I could have ever imagined. I have learnt more about myself in these past few years than ever before. I have learnt more about this world, and everything and everyone in it than ever before.

When I first sat down and created my 'Mindfully Evie' blog and social media accounts, four months into being housebound, I had no idea what I was going to be writing about or if anyone (besides my mum) would read it. Putting that pen to paper for the first time, having the freedom to write whatever was inside of me, I would soon find became a complete love, passion and addiction of mine.

Always writing from a place of happiness and positivity, I wrote about the things I had learnt and the things I was still learning. I offered advice and insight to others into how we can be happy and at peace within ourselves in a world full of suffering. I found that the more I wrote, the more I grew, and the more I grew, the more I wrote. The response I got was incredible. No words can describe how it feels when people tell you that your words pulled them out of a bad day, that your post was everything they needed in that moment, that your writing has inspired them and become a light in their life.

I never set out to be inspirational or wise, and I still don't. I didn't become happy or find peace within these four walls for other people; I did it all for myself. When I write, I simply write what's inside of me. I transfer all of it onto paper, and for some reason or another, it connects to people. It speaks to them. And I've come to learn that's the beauty of being open and vulnerable; you create this open connection to everyone you come across.

So many people ask me how I do it, how I stay so positive, how I can be so happy, especially when I'm so young and ill. It's tough to answer why in one sentence, but I hope this book will help answer that.

# Introduction

## About the book

The title of this book was very obvious to me because I want this book to be a testament to my time being housebound. I'm scared that as I distance myself from these housebound days, I'll distort this period into memories of unbearable hardship, which it isn't. I want to be able to look back at this chapter of my life and see this book as living, breathing proof that despite it all, I was happy and at peace throughout everything.

You'll find this book is a collection of "pieces" (as I like to call them): some longer, some shorter, some reading like letters, others like journal entries, some like poems, and some continuous and broken prose. The book is split into three parts: The Storm, The Aftermath, and The Calm.

When I'm having a bad moment, I often write as a way to come home to myself; to remind myself it is all going to be okay and that this is not the end of my story. This is what the pieces in 'The Storm' are - they are the words I needed to hear to pull myself out of the bad moment. I hope they provide comfort and warmth to you.

'The Aftermath' is the stage that comes after you have gone through, or are still going through, a hard time. The biggest thing that happened to me after I fell ill was I lost all my confidence and self-esteem. This had a huge impact on my life and the relationships with those around me, as well as the relationship I had with myself. This part is about picking yourself back up and putting those broken, or still breaking, pieces back together again.

The final part, 'The Calm', is to offer you inspiration and wisdom as I share the things I have learnt over these past few years. I hope this part is a soothing and uplifting read for you.

While most of this book is based on my life, there are a few pieces based on things that have happened to other people, usually individuals close to me, and I have written the pieces with those people in mind. You'll also find a bonus chapter called 'A Conversation with Wisdom', but I'll let you find out for yourself what that entails.

You can read this book in order, as it will take you on a transformative journey from the bad moments, to the good moments, and everything in between. But you are also welcome to dip in and out of this book depending on how you are feeling at that moment and which part you feel you need to read the most.

**Ending note**

For whatever reason you have chosen to read my book today, I want to say thank you. I hope that whatever you're going through right now, you are able to create moments of happiness, peace, and joy.

Love,

Evie xx

# Part One:

# The Storm

# Within These Four Walls

Opening the windows
I stare into the world around me,
the one I long to be a part of.
It's a world that has become so unfamiliar to me,
it holds a dreamlike quality in my mind.
Is it even real?
For all I know I have made it up,
for it has been too long.
All I know are these four walls:
this is the extent of my world.
Seeing the world out my window,
I feel the crushing weight on my heart;
the pull towards 'out there'.
I long to wake up from this moment where I can run,
run downstairs and out the front door,
out where the grass is underneath my feet,
where people wear shoes,
where adventures start,
where human beings are real-life figures
and not just imaginations of my mind.
But I can't.
This isn't a dream I will wake up from.
This is my reality.
These four walls are my home,
and for now,
they are the extent of my world.
And so I shut my windows and step away from the
view of a world I so long to be a part of,

# The Storm

and whisper to myself as I return back to my bed,
one day I will make it,
one day I will get there.
But for now,
I will let go of the longing and come back to being,
since no good has ever come from dwelling
in the house of longing for too long
as one can forget to live.
So I come back to this moment,
show up for what it has to offer me,
let the storm of heartbreak and loss pass,
and breathe deeply again into the house of being.

NOT THERE YET

There is a life to be lived between rock bottom and fully healed. There is joy to be found and peace to be unearthed even when you're still in the mess of things. There is hope and trust to be felt even when you're not as far along as you thought you would be.

That in-between stage of, "I'm not where I used to be", but, "I'm still not where I want to be", is not a place in your life to be brushed aside and dismissed. It is not a place where life stops happening to you as you idly sit, waiting for the clock to tick by. You don't have to be fully healed or have everything together to be able to live your life fully.

Because through the mess, the ups and downs, the in-betweens, wherever you find yourself, know that life is still with you, and it will never leave you. Life will follow you through everything; the darkness and the light, letting you know it's still there. So no matter what things may look like for you right now, know that there is, and always will be, a life here for you.

# The Storm

I know times are scary right now.
I know you didn't want this to happen to you.
I know you want to go back to your old life.
But hold on tight,
because although you can't see it right now,
things are going to change a whole lot more for you.
Right now you've been planted;
you're underground, and you can't find the light.
That's okay.
You'll grow at your own pace,
in your own time.
But in order to grow
you need to keep nurturing yourself.
Be kind,
be brave,
keep going,
and never give up.
One day you'll grow so high you'll forget what it's like
to be underground.
You'll become this whole new person you never
thought you could be.
So sit tight,
because I promise things are about to get a lot better.

# Within These Four Walls

HONESTY

Trying to hold your broken pieces together,
pretending everything is okay and "fine",
is not productive or good for you.
You are resisting how you are feeling and
the storm that is happening inside of you,
and through this resistance you are
sending a message to yourself that
how you are feeling is wrong.
You are telling yourself it's not okay
to not be okay.

But it is, it really is.

It's okay to fall apart.
It's okay to acknowledge when you're broken.
Because only through your honesty of how
you are feeling and coping right now can you
finally accept just how hard things are.
It is only through this acceptance that
things start to change.

Being honest about how you are feeling
is the starting place for transformation.
It is only from here that you can start to
heal and come back together again.

# The Storm

THE TRUE MEANING OF FRIENDSHIP

Tell me the parts of you that you think are unlovable,
so I can pour my heart into those gaps.
Tell me the parts of you that make you cry,
so I can help you see all the good and wonderful
things in yourself.
Tell me the parts of you that hurt,
so I can hold your hand through the suffering.
Tell me the parts of you that break your heart,
so I can stand by your side as you stitch it back
together.
Tell me the parts of you that make you feel ashamed,
so I can share my insecurities with you too.
Tell me the parts of you that you think no one
understands,
so I can offer you a person who will listen deeply.
Tell me the parts of you that you have buried deep
under the surface in shame,
so I can give you a non-judgmental space to open up
in.
Tell me the parts of you where people have mistreated
you,
so I can remind you of your worth.
And after all that, after you have given me your real,
your all, your everything;
you'll find I'm still right here next to you.

# Within These Four Walls

ONE STEP

When you feel you have so far to go,
remember that the future does not yet exist,
and that time only truly exists
in the present moment.
These steps you are yet to climb
only exist in your mind,
for right in this moment
you do not need to start climbing.
All you need to do
is breathe;
this moment is all you have
and is all you need.
Cast those future steps away
and stay in the here and now.
You will get there,
but right now
you are not required
to think of the height.
Just this moment,
just this next small step forward,
is all you ever need to think about.

# The Storm

Lost to who she was,
she stumbles through the darkness
trying to find pieces of the person
she used to be,
which only a moment ago
she lost to the
oncoming wave of sadness
and grief,
pulling her under
until she forgot how to reach the surface.
Here in the darkness,
she can't remember
the purpose of this.
The thoughts of giving up
creep into her mind,
swirling around trying to
pull her further under.
But the person who she
used to be is still there.
Trying to get back to her,
she hears it through the cracks and occasional silence,
telling her to be brave,
to come back to the surface,
to never stop kicking against the tide,
to never give up.
Hearing the voice of the person
she used to be
gives her

enough strength,
enough courage,
to say
'I'm coming,
I'm coming home to myself.'

Don't ever give up.
Don't ever give up.
Don't ever give up.

# The Storm

IS THIS IT?

When you have those moments where you start to think, is this it? Is this all there is to life? Know that this hollow feeling is temporary, and everyone feels it once in a while. There is so much more to life than what you feel in this moment. Remember all the times you made the world a better place, in the smallest and most significant ways, merely by being in it.

You have changed people's lives by simply loving them. You have given pieces of yourself to loved ones merely so they could flourish. You have spoken words that provided a person comfort in a time of need. You have done something for someone just so you could see them smile. You have made people laugh, and you have brought people joy.

There are people in this
world whose happiness
has expanded because of
you. Think of that when
you start to wonder
what life is all about.

HEAVY

You stand so strong
despite the load you carry.
Your grace
and attitude
with the way you move
through your heaviness
is awe-inspiring.
But it's okay
if you need
to stop,
to rest awhile.
Just because you carry it well
does not mean
you do not still
feel the weight.
Breathe deeply
into this moment
when it all feels
too much to bear.
You are doing so well,
you have been so brave,
and you have come so far.
When you feel ready
to continue ahead,
go with
a softness
and a light
guiding you.

# The Storm

But before you get
back up again,
sit and reflect
on your journey,
and take pride
in all the moments
you got through
to reach this moment.
Gather the strength
you need in these
thoughts and reflections,
and know it is okay
to sit here
and rest
for a while.

Slow

And here you are, trying so hard to get to where you want to be, putting in all these hours and endless days of effort, when someone who hasn't given half as much effort or time as you rushes right past. They go on to achieve everything you've ever dreamed of with seamlessly effortless grace and ease, and here you are, still toiling away, your progress seemingly small in comparison.

It doesn't seem fair, and it often isn't. But you have to remember, their journey is not your journey. It may seem like they have overtaken you, it may seem like they are doing what you're doing more successfully. But the outward progress is so slight in comparison to the inward growth, and that is what you can't see. You can't compare yourself to this person because you cannot see the whole picture of their progress.

They may have flaunted past you now, but a few years down the line they might be back to where they started. Or maybe they won't be. Perhaps they simply got lucky. But don't let their success make you feel you are doing something wrong. Don't let their progress and speed make you feel heavy-hearted about yours. You are still moving forward, and there is growth in that. It may take you a long time to get there, but maybe this is because you are on a path that must not be rushed.

Trust that you will still get there, and trust that this slow process is because great things take time. Don't be off-put by the speed or progress of others. This is your path, and it cannot belong to anyone else; it was meant only for you. You are creating something beautiful through this slow movement, and you will still get to where you want to be. There is no rush when it comes to growth. Take your time.

# Within These Four Walls

YOU STILL BELONG HERE

You think you are forgotten here
behind these four walls,
but you are not.

You think your life is worth less
than those whose lives live
in the world out there,
but it is not.

You were not brought
into this world by accident.
You were meant to be here.
Whether that be confined to
this room or the whole world.
Whether your life is
limited or limitless.
Whether you can
believe it or not.

You are still,
and always will be,
meant to be here
in this world.

# The Storm

A PROMISE

Another day is ending,
another day you've made it through.
You are growing,
you are breathing,
you are going to make it.
This is not the end of your story.

# Within These Four Walls

I know it sometimes feels like life is happening
without you, but it's not.
You know deep down it's not.
Your life is still happening, right here, right now.
Writing these words proves your life is not being
wasted.
You're learning. You're growing.
Life is still happening to you even if it is different
from everyone else's.
There is no set path everyone has to go down for life
to happen, so don't try to change anything.
Don't force something to be different from what it
already is.
Because this is it, this is your life, and you can't
change that.
It doesn't have to be bad, nor does it have to be
something spectacular; it can just be.
Make the most of this time because it is a luxury most
people don't get and an opportunity for growth that
you don't want to miss.
Life will still happen with or without you – only you
can decide whether to go with it or resist it.
It may still be different from everyone else's life and
not the one you had in mind – but who is to say it
isn't better?

# The Storm

YOU STILL MADE IT

And even when you feel
that this day has been wasted,
that nothing is changing,
that you are stuck in an endless
cycle of loss and grief.
Remember,
you have shown strength,
by getting through the days
you never thought you'd get through.
You have shown courage,
by showing up each day,
even when you thought
you couldn't go on anymore.
You have been so brave
to make it this far.
Don't give up now.
You will get there,
you will make it,
and you will be alright.

# Within These Four Walls

HEALING TAKES TIME

As these days tick by
inside these four walls,
nothing you say
seems to change.
But have you not noticed
all the changes around you,
and all the changes within you?
As small as they may be,
for subtlety is their middle name,
do not belittle them for their size.
As over time these little changes,
stone by stone,
will grow into mountains.

# The Storm

I HOPE YOU REMEMBER

On the days when you begin to doubt your progress,
I hope you remember just how far you have come.
On the days when you tell yourself to pull it together,
I hope you remember it's okay to fall apart.
On the days when it feels like everything is going
wrong,
I hope you remember all the times that it has gone
right.
On the days when the end seems so far,
I hope you remember to breathe deeply and to take it
one moment at a time.
On the days when you don't feel enough,
I hope you remember you are already whole and to
always be kind to yourself.
On the days when everything feels too much,
I hope you remember this feeling will pass.

OLD MYTH

Bravery,
has too often been confused
with swords
and knights in shining armour.
When bravery
should be about
facing your fears,
not fighting them.
Surrendering to the fear,
surrendering to the pain,
surrendering to the sadness,
surrendering to the moment.
This is bravery.
For you cannot be brave
if you are not afraid.
So put down your sword
and let your fears in.

# The Storm

YOU CAN STILL BE AT PEACE WHEN YOU'RE
UNDERGROUND

Whoever told you that you have to like
where you are to be happy is mistaken.
You do not have to like where you are.
You do not even have to pretend that you do.
Because even then you can still choose to focus on
everything you have.
To focus on what you have gained.
To focus on the growth,
the light,
and the good.
To trust,
to breathe,
to accept.
In this place,
you did not want or care to be,
you can still choose to feel peace and
create your happiness from within.
It will be harder than most,
and require practise and patience,
but it is so very possible.
I promise you,
from the darkness of my bedroom
as I write these words,
it is possible.

THERE IS ALWAYS CHANGE

When you live life in the slow lane, it can often feel like all the days merge into one. It becomes hard to differentiate between them as all the days seem exactly the same: the same routine, the same activities, the same emotions, the same rest periods. There isn't much room for spontaneity or eventful activities which break up the days and unfortunately routine is often vital for recovery. But it is important to remember that while the days seem to blend together, they are always different.

The days may all start with a sunrise and end with a sunset, yet no sky is ever the same. The days may be filled with moments of the same emotions: happiness, frustration, grief, joy, contentment, yet your experience of each emotion is always different from the last. The days may embody the same surroundings and scenery inside, yet outside the weather and garden are forever changing. The days may be a repeat of the same routines and the same journeys, yet each day, your thoughts and emotions during these moments will continuously differ, making it a new experience each time. The days may feel like they are on constant repeat, with nothing moving or altering, yet today you are a day older, a day wiser, and a day more knowledgeable. Each day is always different. Notice the changes each day brings and appreciate each one as it comes as there won't be another day like the one today.

# The Storm

ROCK BOTTOM

Some people need to fall apart first
because only when they're broken
completely can they
finally see and
accept just
how
far
they
have
fallen.
It is only
through the
fall that they realise
how much they don't
want to live like this anymore,
and only then do they find the
motivation to build themselves back up again.

NOTEBOOK SCRIBBLES #2: YOU ARE GROWING FROM
THIS

You can do this. You've got this. You will get there.
Stop comparing where you are now to this time last
year. You are so different and so far from the place
you were a year ago.
Last year you didn't have the emotional and mental
strength that you have now.
Last year you were born again, learning to walk on
new legs.
This year you have an entire year of life experience to
guide you.
You didn't know what to do this time last year, but
you know what you have to do now.
From the outside, you may look as if you are in
exactly the same place, but you know deep down just
how vastly different the two places are.
A year ago feels like a different lifetime.
You may have relapsed again, and your physical
health is back to rock bottom, but this time around it
already feels so different.
You're on solid ground now; it's not going to
crumble, it's only going to get stronger.
Your health may not have improved, but you have.
Hold on to that.
You are growing from this.

# The Storm

FREE

A heart a little heavier,
the day passing by a little slower.
Thoughts of open roads,
blue skies,
adventures,
and scenes of breathtaking beauty
that she has only seen in pictures
flash through her mind.
A longing to be anywhere
but this house,
this room,
dominate her heart.
Even the garden,
where she can feel the grass beneath her feet
and look up into the open sky,
would feel like a palace right now
compared to this room
she has been stuck in
for six months.
One day she asks,
can I not have one day off from all of this?
One day of freedom,
one day to do anything I want.
But of course,
it isn't that easy.
Because this is not something
she can just switch off.
It is not something she has

the luxury to take a break from.
It is something she has to live with
throughout every inhale and exhale.

One day she will know what it
means to live without all this.
One day she will know what it
means to be free.

But for now, live with it she will.
And she will live with it so beautifully.
She will brave this day one inhale at a time,
and she knows she'll be okay.

Because every day
that passes brings her
closer to where she
really wants to be,
and one day soon
she will finally see,
what it feels like to
live fully and be free.

# The Storm

What is suffering but the absence of joy?
And what is joy but the absence of suffering?
The two so connected and intertwined;
as one sets the other will rise.
And like the seasons of summer and winter,
there will be periods
when the darkness of suffering is more prolonged,
and the light of joy is fleeting.
But just as it is never winter all year round,
summer will come once again,
and the darkness of suffering will retreat
as the light of joy stretches longer into your days.
Yet to wish to have one without the other is
impossible.
You cannot have summer without winter.
You cannot have light without dark.
Accept that they are bound together,
and let them each rise and fall of their own accord
as they continuously take their turns to dip in and
out of your life.
And remind yourself in the light of joy,
that this feeling would not be possible if you
had not first lived through the darkness of suffering.
And remember in the darkness of suffering,
that the light of joy will always rise once again.

A HEART A LITTLE HEAVIER

When you have been through so much, you will always carry a heart a little heavier. You will feel hurt deeper than other people because it will remind you of all the hurt you have been through before. You will feel emotions stronger than other people because you have already experienced emotions that run so deep. You might take things more seriously than other people because you have been through things that tested everything you have.

But with this heart a little heavier, you will find you have room to enjoy life a bit deeper too. You will be able to love people harder and have more to offer them because there is so much more inside of you to give. You will be able to feel a happiness that bit deeper because all that darkness you have gotten through will make the light times that much brighter. You will hold more compassion and kindness for others because you feel and understand their pain more clearly.

You may wish your heart was not as heavy, that you could take things less seriously, that your emotions were not felt as fully, but all these things will lead you to live a life that bit more profound. You will create joy out of things most people overlook. You will find a connection to yourself and the world more abundant and fulfilled. You will find meaning in every breath and step you take.

And all these things cannot be bought or taken away from you; they only happened to you through experience, so make the most of what this heavy heart offers you. Allow it to show you that because of everything that has been, you now get to live a deeper life filled with a little more love, clarity, and meaning.

NOTEBOOK SCRIBBLES #3: RESPONSE

My heart is telling me to trust my journey,
to be patient,
to breathe,
to take it one moment at a time.
But my head wants answers,
for it does not understand something
it cannot see.
As time goes on my head keeps interfering,
and I keep having to drag myself back to that place in
my heart of patience and trust.
But I do,
and I'll keep doing it,
for as long and however many times it takes.
Because no matter what happens
I get to choose how I respond to this,
and I will always choose to live from
a place of love,
patience,
and trust.

The Storm

## BEAUTY

And even with all the suffering
that surrounds her,
she will find beauty in each moment.

✦

## THE LITTLE THINGS

No matter what happens to you in life,
there is always something to be grateful for
and something to smile about.

✦

## HEALING MANTRA

I shall stay patient and trust my journey.

✦

## BEST FRIEND

"I'm sorry we always have to leave you on
your own," they said, "It must be so lonely."

Turning to look at her four-legged friend,
she replied, "I'm not alone. I'm never alone."

# Within These Four Walls

I HOPE YOU FIND THE COURAGE

I hope from this moment forward
you will find the courage
to do all those things
you have been too afraid of...

To those of you
who have kept running to hide from
the storm that's happening inside of you:
I hope you find the courage
to stand still and face it without judgement.

To those of you
who have ignored
your pain for so long:
I hope you find the courage to acknowledge
and embrace your pain with compassion.

To those of you
who are scared to be
alone with your thoughts:
I hope you find the courage
to learn you are not your thoughts,
and that everything that lives in
your mind is only temporary.

To those of you
who have stepped back
into the space of comfort,

## The Storm

too afraid to move forward:
I hope you find the courage
to take that leap into
the unexplored and unknown
with a heart full of curiosity and wonder.

To those of you
who are putting something off
out of a lack of self-belief:
I hope you find the courage
to believe in yourself
and to realise you should
fear regret more than you
should fear failure.

To those of you
who are wondering
whether to take that risk:
I hope you find the courage
to realise life is too short
to not give it your all.

HOLD ONTO HOPE

Hope does wonders for the soul.
It's the thing that gives you light in the dark.
It's the thing that makes you put one foot in front of
the other even when you can't see what's ahead.
It's the thing that tells you things will get better.
It's the thing that makes even the hardest times just
that little bit softer, easier, and more bearable.
It's the thing that keeps you going when times are so
tough.

Hope is one of those things you don't know how much
you need it until you realise you don't have it. One of
the best ways to feel hope is knowing there are people
who have got through what you're going through. To
know that others have been where you are now but are
currently doing so much better.

To read about people who have found peace and
happiness amid their suffering. To hear those people
say how far they've come. To see others achieving
things they once believed weren't possible.

Hold onto the fact that if they got through it, then so
can you.

# The Storm

Whenever I feel regrets about my past
or overwhelmed with emotion
when it comes back to haunt me in the dark,
I will remind myself it is because of my past
that I got to be the person I am today.
I will not let it hold me back,
but instead,
let it propel me forward.
I will let go of the sadness and shame
it still causes me,
but hold on tightly to the lessons
it taught me.
I'm thankful for all of it,
but I am ready to move on.

# Within These Four Walls

## YOU DON'T NEED TO EXPLAIN IT

Feeling sad for no reason is still a valid reason.

✦

## THE FIRST STEP

You cannot let go of something
if you have not first acknowledged its
presence and accepted its existence.

✦

## IT'S OKAY

Grasping her sadness with both hands,
she embedded it within her heart,
embraced it with love
and said, "It's okay,
it's all going to be okay."

✦

## THE RIGHT ATMOSPHERE

Stillness and quiet:
the perfect feeding ground for healing.

# The Storm

GOES BOTH WAYS

I waited for the "something special"
and wouldn't settle for less.
I waited for someone to come into my life
and for me to realise,
this is it,
this is the one I want and have waited for.
This is the person I want to spend
the rest of my life with.
I turned away 99%,
I was holding out for the 100;
the one I had no doubts about.
What I didn't consider,
what I never saw coming,
was that you wouldn't feel the same way for me.
How could I be so naive?
How could I overlook something so huge?
I assumed if I waited for the right person,
it would be a given that I was
the right person for them too.
And now you're gone from my life,
I'm left broken.
But I'll remind myself
you couldn't have been the one for me,
because you would still be here if you were.
So as I knit my broken pieces back together again,
I'll tell myself to keep looking
because you weren't it.
I won't let you stop me from believing

that when I find another who I feel
is the one for me once more,
I will be the one for them too.
And maybe then
that's when I should realise,
this is what I held out for.
This is it.
You're not just meant for me,
but I was also meant for you too.

# The Storm

IT'S OKAY TO GO UNDER

Do not feel ashamed
you are not handling all this pain
with grace or dignity.
You will learn and grow from this,
but maybe not at the moment.
For when there is so much pain and darkness,
you often need to go through it
before you can grow from it.

DENYING LIFE

What do you do when you lose the life you built everything to get? When the life you had was so perfect for you. What do you do when you lose that life overnight? As much as you try to listen to all those who tell you to accept the life you now have, to be grateful for everything you can still do, your old life is like a tug of the soul pulling you away from this moment back into a past you can no longer reach.

But can you not see, by longing for a life you no longer have, by turning your back on this moment, you deny life itself? Because you are only alive at this moment. You are not living by replaying those moments from the past: you are remembering.

No, maybe this life won't be as good as what you had. And no, perhaps it isn't what you want. But that isn't to say you can't still experience moments of pure joy and peace, and those moments are absolutely everything.

Your life has not stopped, you have just stopped living. Because whether you are ready to accept it or not, this is your life now, and you can't change that. Life will always be walking alongside you: all you have to do is decide whether or not to step back in and join it.

# The Storm

WAITING ZONE

You are allowed to hope
that there is something
more for you,
waiting on your road ahead,
than what this moment offers.
Whilst at the same time,
understanding that while you wait,
there is always peace
to be found here
and a life to be lived.

You can both hope
that the future is better
and yet still be happy
with everything you have
at this moment.

COURAGE

Courage is...

Learning to be vulnerable,
when you are told to be strong.
Learning to accept your flaws,
when you are told to be perfect.
Learning to surrender to the pain,
when you are told this is weak.
Learning to speak out,
when you are told to be silent.
Learning to trust the uncertainty,
when you are told to plan.
Learning to go your own way,
when you are told there is only one path.

This is courage.

# The Storm

BAD MOMENTS STILL HAPPEN TO STRONG PEOPLE

Today it feels like everything is falling apart.
It feels like those stones you built into mountains
where you sit are crumbling beneath you.
But this tremble you feel only lies within you;
it does not affect the mountain
you have so carefully built.
When you stop shaking,
you will look out and see you're just as high up
as you were before the tremble.
And getting through this moment,
take pride knowing you can
now add another stone
to your mountain and
stand even higher.

BLINDED BY HOPE

Time,
melting away so fast in this room.
Like grains of sand
slipping through my fingers,
unable to understand where it all went.
You'd think time would tick by slowly,
with little to do
and nowhere to go.
But with so few hours in the day,
so many hours consumed to
the call of rest,
it slithers by.
Tomorrow you say,
tomorrow will be better,
and yet before you know it,
tomorrow has come and gone.
Another day lost to false hope.
Clinging to the fact that one of these days to come
surely must be better.
One of these days
I must experience a day full of life and energy.
Blinded by hope,
days, months, and years go by,
holding on to the thought,
that maybe tomorrow will be better.

# The Storm

Where you currently are is not permanent.
You may only be in this place for a short while, or
you may be here a little longer than you hoped.
You may enjoy where you are, or maybe you haven't
enjoyed it for a long time.
You may feel there is so much more you can offer to
the world.
You may resist this place and believe you shouldn't be
here.
Or maybe this place feels right.
Maybe you can see the magic and growth happening
from this place.
But whether you like where you are right now or not,
this is where you are.
Just for now.
Just temporarily.
Because before you know it, you'll move on to a new
place, and maybe the place you move on to will be the
place you really want to be.
But let's not waste this place where you are now by
waiting for the next one.
Because before you know it, you'll be moving along to
somewhere new, as everything is always temporary.

REST

It takes great strength and courage to stop and rest. Why? Because we have been taught our whole lives that we should be busy. That to rest is counterproductive and futile. That slowing down is a sign of weakness.

So when we fall sick, we struggle to grasp this concept that rest is a good thing. That healing occurs during the times we rest, much more so than the times we push ourselves.

But by needing to stop and rest, it can often be a heavy reminder that your body cannot do what other healthy bodies can do. That you cannot keep up with others and the speed they live their lives at. And that's so so tough. It's such a hard realisation to face when all you want is to join in with everyone and be "normal" for a while.

I hope you remember during these moments that although resting may feel unproductive, it is the complete opposite of that. You are not "wasting time" or having "a lazy day" by resting – you are healing. You are planting seeds for recovery. You are putting your body first and giving it what it needs at this moment. You are doing all these things right now so one day you will be able to join in and do all those things everyone else is doing – because you will get there.

# The Storm

sting becomes too hard for you to do, when
e temptation to push through instead of
stopping and listening to your body's needs, I hope you
remember to remind yourself:

> Rest because you want to get better,
> not because you're sick.

✦

> In this space of rest, you are planting seeds
> for recovery and healing.

✦

> Even if some days all you can do is lie in bed
> and rest – that's okay. You're still doing a "thing"
> even if it doesn't always feel like it.

✦

> You are not weak for needing to rest –
> you are strong for recognising and giving
> what your mind and body require.

# Within These Four Walls

## THE WAY OUT

Health goes downhill
↓
Feels helpless and overcome with sadness about this*
↓
Negativity drains energy
↓
Health goes downhill...


*Acknowledges sadness and helplessness with open
arms
↓
Wraps oneself in self-compassion and love
↓
Stays focused on staying in the present moment to avoid
overthinking and catastrophizing
↓
Holds onto hope and trust that everything will be okay
↓
Seeks out the peace, calm, and stillness this moment
offers
↓
Focuses on the good things in life and finds joy and
gratitude in the little things

# The Storm

LETTING GO OF RESISTANCE

Ten steps back,
still no steps forward.
She wants to move
but a barricade blocks her
to where she wants to go.
She cannot figure out why
this barricade is there or
what she has to do to beat it.
She tries everything
and yet nothing works.
Frustrated,
she kicks,
hits,
screams,
and cries.
Temporarily defeated,
confused,
exhausted,
she knows something needs to change,
but she still cannot move forward.
So that's when it occurs to her
to stop and look at the spot where she is now.
It's not where she wants to be,
but maybe it's not as bad as it first seemed.
Feeling hopeful,
she sits.
For she knows the barricade will one day lift,
whether through time or effort

she does not know.
But she has seen it lift for other people,
so therefore knows one day it'll happen to her,
and then she'll finally be free to move forward.
But for now
she has an opportunity
to practise peace and happiness
at the spot where she's stuck.
So she sits,
and she waits,
as patiently as can be,
knowing one day
she'll make it.
But for now,
this spot will have to do.
Because even on the bottom step
she knows,
peace can be attained,
and happiness is still achievable.

# The Storm

FALSE HOPE

No matter how many times
our heart has been broken
by the beacon of hope
that things are finally getting better,
only for the curtain to drop and reveal
in the cruellest manner
it was merely an illusion,
we cannot help but fall for the light again
each time we see it.

UNBOUND AT SEA

Trapped here in the sea,
with nothing that can ground me,
I found an ease with letting things be,
instead of always trying to flee.

Now unbound,
I jumped and took a leap,
discovering things
I would never have learnt
had I not been flung into the deep.

So here I am,
learning to ride the wave,
knowing that this is brave.

And that even in the sea,
with no guarantee,
you can still live a life
and know what it feels like
to live fully and be free.

# The Storm

SITTING IN THE UNCERTAINTY

You don't always have to know why everything happens the way it does. You don't always need to question what this means, what reason is behind it, or what will become of it. You are allowed to sit and rest in the uncertainty.

It can be exhausting always trying to find a reason behind all the suffering. Maybe, you should allow yourself to be okay with not knowing for a little while. To just accept this is how things are, this is what is happening, and being okay with that. To let go of questioning everything that is happening to you and around you, and know that maybe one day you will understand.

Maybe one day you will wake up and think this is why. This is why those years happened to me. And maybe one day all of this will make sense: the hurt, the sadness, the grief. A light will shine upon it all and that weight that has been on your shoulders for so long will be lifted. But you don't need to worry about that right now, because that day will come when it is ready. Let it come to you, and be okay sitting in the uncertainty for a while.

M.E AWARENESS

So many words to write,
too little energy.
So many dreams to conquer,
too little energy.
So many passions to pursue,
too little energy.
So much love to give,
too little energy.
So many countries to see,
too little energy.
So many people to meet,
too little energy.
So many memories to make,
too little energy.
So much life to give,
too little energy.

# The Storm

Just breathe.
Let's take it one moment at a time.
You don't need to work out your entire life just yet.
We have ages, let's go slow.
The only moment that matters is now.
The future doesn't exist, it is an illusion, not reality.
Your anxiety about tomorrow is unnecessary.
Your worry about how life will turn out is pointless.
Smile, life is good.
You just need to breathe.
Stay focused on the now – don't get lost in the future.
Let the words flow across this page as they come,
don't overthink anything, just be.
Be like water, always going with the flow.
You and these words are all it needs to be right now.
So let's just breathe and stay focused on now.

# Within These Four Walls

THERE IS NO CEILING

When you feel you've outgrown
this place you're stuck at.
When you feel you have learnt all
the lessons you needed to learn here.
When you feel you have done your healing
and now you are ready to move on,
but still, you're not getting anywhere.
Take heart that this feeling alone is
forcing you to stand taller than before.
You are still growing,
some more and more each day.
You may not be moving forward,
and you may have no control over this,
but my darling,
no ceiling will ever hold you down.
You are still growing taller each day,
and you will always be allowed to
keep growing some more
while you wait here.

# The Storm

SELF-COMPASSION BLANKET

When the:
"I am not where I should be",
"I should be further along than this",
"This year was supposed to be better",
start to arise in your mind,
I hope in these moments you take care
to treat yourself kindly.
You did not choose this.
You did not choose to be here.
But you are doing the best you can,
and that is always enough.
Go easy on yourself;
take that self-compassion blanket
down from the shelf and wrap
yourself deep inside it.
Allow your body and soul to rest here
in the stillness and warmth for a while.
Tell yourself you will get there.
Tell yourself you will make it.
Tell yourself it will all be okay.
Because you will get there,
you will make it,
and it really is all going to be okay.

MISSING OUT

I'm sorry you're missing out on so much. I'm sorry that while you're stuck here, everyone else is moving on in life and doing all the things you can only dream of. I'm sorry the joy you see in others, the laughter you hear outside, you cannot feel within yourself.

This isn't forever though. How you are feeling isn't forever. This place you're stuck at isn't forever. Even if you can't feel it, you are moving forward, you are growing in ways that maybe you simply can't see right now. But that doesn't mean it isn't happening.

While you think you've been missing out on life, life has still been happening and growing inside of you, waiting for the day it can bloom and show you everything you've been waiting for. Maybe you're missing out right now because the universe is getting ready to show you things not even you could have dreamed. Perhaps this has all been planned – this temporary halt, so when you bloom, you bloom so high.

I know you would rather not miss out. I know you would rather be able to feel the joy you can only see and live the life others are living. But it is coming for you, it is all coming for you. And in the meantime, maybe instead of thinking about how you're missing out on what others are doing, think about how they're missing out on what you're doing. You are growing in ways unimaginable. You are preparing yourself for a life so beautiful. You are gaining a perspective and insight so deep. You are transforming in more ways than one. How lucky you are to experience these things right now, and how lucky you are to know you'll experience all the other things in the future too.

# Within These Four Walls

HOPE

One day,
these days will seem like a faraway dream.
You'll think,
did I really have so little energy I couldn't sit in a
chair,
see my friends or family,
or leave the house for years?
It will all seem like a blur,
and it will feel like a different lifetime.
Because one day you will be in a place so far from
where you are now.
You will be travelling the world,
walking whenever and wherever you want,
spending time with the people you love,
living life to the full.
But something you will never ever forget,
is what these days taught you.
You will never forget the lessons you learnt.
You will never forget how you overcame the struggles.
You will never forget how you grew despite the
circumstances.
You will never forget how you conquered the world
each day simply by getting through it.
You will hold this in your heart for always.
And you will look back and realise,
these days weren't the end,
they weren't a waste of time,
because really,

## The Storm

they were just the beginning,
of a journey so so beautiful
you won't see it coming.
And for that,
you will always be grateful
that these days happened to you.

# Part Two:

# The Aftermath

YOU ARE WORTHY

I'm sorry that all those people left you when you did nothing wrong other than the fact you are unable to leave the house and join in with them. I'm sorry for the pain others have caused you by not understanding just how hard things are for you right now and for making you feel that you are not enough. I'm sorry someone made you feel so very small and insignificant, like you didn't matter and that the world could go on without you.

But you should know this. The pain others have caused you, all those who have made you feel unloved, unworthy, or incomplete: you are none of those things. It may hurt you deeply because you secretly feel that way about yourself too. But you are whole, you are loveable, you are complete. You have nothing to prove to anyone; you have nothing to prove to yourself. You came into this world worthy of all the love, kindness, and affection the universe could offer, and no circumstance or person can and will ever change that.

I hope you let those people's words pass through you and do not allow them to linger in your soul. I hope you see that those people who left you did you a favour by leaving, as they gave you the room for another, better and more loving person to come into your life and take their place. I hope you know that you do matter, you do belong here, and you are worthy of so much more than what those people gave to you.

IN-BETWEEN

Give yourself time to breathe
between the moments
when one relationship ends
and another begins.
Give yourself time
to go back to being
okay by yourself again.
The absence you feel
in your heart
after someone has left
is normal.
But don't go rushing
to fill that void
with another person.
Fill that gap
with your own love,
your own warmth,
your own support.
Give yourself time
to adjust
going back to one,
and let the next person
find you whole.

# The Aftermath

HIGHEST DUTY

Why do we think
the highest praise to give someone
is that they always put others
before themselves?
Have we all forgotten
the highest of all duties?
The duty to care and nourish oneself.
Do you not think you owe yourself that?
Before giving to others
and leaving your own soul bare.

MISSING

I feel like there's something
missing inside of me today,
not allowing me to feel
quite as whole
or at peace
as I usually do.
But maybe nothing is missing,
and that's the problem.
Maybe it's the belief that I feel
I lack something
that is causing me
to feel a little less than whole.
Maybe it's because while I've been
searching for answers,
I should have been staying here
in this moment.
Because here I can see
that wholeness comes
from the belief and realisation
that nothing is ever missing;
I already have everything I need.
So I let go of searching
for what's missing and
come back to the present moment,
where I find everything I need.

# The Aftermath

CONFIDENCE

Confidence can be a slippery thing.
Just when we think we've got it in our grasp
one word from another and our confidence
can shatter into a thousand pieces.
Then piece by piece,
we slowly start putting it back together again,
before another comes along and
utters another bad word,
causing the ball of confidence
to slip from our hands and smash.
And thus, the cycle continues.

When we will ever understand
our own approval
is the only one that should matter?
When will we ever learn
our own approval
should be enough?

CONFIDENCE MANTRA

Believe in who you are.
Believe in what you do.
Believe in yourself.

✦

## DREAMS

It's okay to aim high; to have your dreams as tall as
the stars and as vast as the ocean. Why? Because you
won't get anywhere if you always aim for the floor.

✦

THE INTERNET

Don't ever let someone else's false opinion of you
make you question how incredible you are.

✦

DON'T FORGET

Just because someone is doing something
you are not, does not make what they are doing
better than what you're doing.

# The Aftermath

The things that don't define you as a person:

- Your qualifications.
- Your health or illness.
- Numbers in a bank account.
- Your relationship status.
- Your exam results.
- Your list of physical achievements.
- Your gender, race, sexuality, or physical appearance.
- External circumstances not within your control.

The things that do:

- How you treat your friends and family.
- How you treat strangers.
- How you treat yourself.
- The energy you put out in the universe.
- How you make other people feel.
- Your attitude in life.
- How kind you are.
- Your morals and beliefs.
- The care you show for the planet.
- Who you are as an individual.

EMPTY SHELL

As she held close to his body
he gave her love and a home in return.
But it didn't take long
for the love he gave her to cease.
Forgetting she could let go,
she clung to his empty shell,
pouring in everything she had
in the hope
that he would one day
return the love
she was giving him.
But the love never came.
She was too afraid
to let go of his shell,
for it was once so familiar and warm;
it felt like home.
If only she knew
an empty shell
is not home.
So let go
and pour the love
you were giving away,
back into yourself.
For this body is your home.

# The Aftermath

There will be so many times in your life where you put all your energy and effort into something only to get nothing back. To work hard at a relationship to stop it from breaking. To work hard at trying to prove to someone, you are more than what they think you are. To work hard at a treatment that is draining everything you have. And even after all this work, these endless hours of effort you have put in, it has made no difference.

You may want to keep going, to keep putting your energy into it, thinking, just a little bit more, just a little bit more time and effort, and then it will change, then it will all be worth it for something. And maybe it will, perhaps then it will all be worthwhile. But a lot of the time it isn't. A lot of the time we can give our everything and still get nothing back.

It is during these times you need to think if it is still worth giving it your energy, or is it best just to walk away. To walk away, knowing nothing has come of it even after everything, but knowing the energy you have left is better spent on yourself and moving on. Walking away from something or someone even if you feel you still have something left to give, but knowing that giving that little part of you left simply might not be worth it and might be better spent on yourself.

It's so hard to walk away from something when you have invested so much time and effort. It is so hard to walk away from something with the knowledge that maybe there is still a chance, with even more effort and time, that things could change. But even with that possibility, and even with the disappointment that nothing has changed, it doesn't always give enough of a reason to stay. Take that last bit of energy you have and give it to yourself. Give it to yourself so you can walk away and move on to better things.

# The Aftermath

NOTHING TO PROVE

You are still worthy and deserving of love, from both yourself and others, even if you do not meet the demands and expectations the world puts on your shoulders.

✦

YOU DON'T NEED OTHERS TO GIVE YOU THE A-OKAY

The phrase 'seeking approval' should not mean to seek approval from others, but to seek approval of oneself. Because when you have your own approval, you are freed from the burden of needing approval from others, and this is when you are at your most powerful.

✦

YOU HOLD ALL THE PIECES

You are still whole without another person standing by your side. So even if in their absence you feel they took something from you when they left, know that everything you need is already inside of you. They cannot have taken something that did not belong to them in the first place.

COMFORT ZONE

I dream of travelling the world solo;
with no set destination,
no return journey home,
because I know,
despite the fear I will face
as I step out of my comfort zone,
this is where I will grow.
I know that
the uncomfortable
is the path to be
taken often,
as only when we're on the edge
do we truly learn things
about ourselves
and the world
that we never knew before
in the safety of our home.
It does not make you fearless
taking these leaps;
you are allowed to be terrified
of the jump
you are about to take.
But know in your heart
you need this path
as much as it needs you.

# The Aftermath

There are some people in life who you might still cling onto because letting go of them means letting go of the person you used to be. They might be the only thing you have left from your old life or the only person who knows who you were before all of this. And you don't want to let them go, because you're not ready to give up that identity. Clinging to them feels like the only way you can keep the old you alive and to let go of them would be to throw yourself into the deep end; to finally accept that your old life and the person you used to be is no longer here.

But by clinging onto them, you are not even giving this new life or this new you a chance. You are dragging things back out from the past that are no longer meant to be here. You are trying to pretend nothing has changed and you are resisting what has happened. And yet things change, all the time, and no matter how much you try and pull your old identity back up from the ground, once it's uprooted, you can't replant it. Once you've seen the world in a new way, no matter how hard you try, you can't go back to the way you saw the world before.

So even though you want to cling to this person, you want to keep hold of your old identity, your old life, all you are doing is trying to keep hold of something that is no longer meant to be here. Although it can be so so hard, you need to let go. You need to let your old identity go. You need to let that person who reminds you of your old life go. Because only when you do this, only when you finally embrace the change that has happened to you, can you then start to see the beauty in things again.

There are no words that can truly describe the feeling that comes with finally letting go of all the things that you've held onto for so long; something between freedom and breathing, you will feel lighter than you've been in such a long time.

# The Aftermath

## GUT FEELING

That thing you feel
pulling you towards
one direction
instead of the other:
it's called intuition.
Listen to it.

❖

## NO REASON

It's okay to walk away from someone
even if there is no reason or red flag,
but simply the fact they make you feel
something a little less than whole.

❖

## DON'T LET OTHERS MAKE YOU QUESTION YOURSELF

When someone plants seeds
of self-doubt in your mind,
pluck them straight out
and hand them back.

BE SENSITIVE

I don't want you to tell me I can achieve anything I set my mind to – I want you to tell me that what I'm doing is already enough.

I don't want you to tell me I have the power to change my life – I want you to see that if I had the power to change my life, my life would not be what it is.

I don't want you to tell me everything happens for a reason – because right now, I'm struggling to see the reason.

I don't want you to tell me I shouldn't feel sad – I want you to tell me that whatever I'm feeling is okay and understandable.

I want you to realise just how little control I have over my situation and be proud of me that despite all that, I'm still here living and growing, choosing to live my life as best and as fully as I can. I want you to shout to me from the rooftops that my best is always enough, and that's all anyone can ever give in life.

# The Aftermath

DEAD END

Why do you stay with someone
who you see no future with,
only for it to end in hurt and heartbreak?
Would it not be better
to avoid romantic entanglement and
use this time to figure out who you are by yourself?
You have your whole life ahead of you
to spend it with another person.
Don't waste these opportunities
for growth and discovery
by spending it with someone
simply to pass the time.
Dedicate these moments to cultivating
a loving relationship with yourself
and focus on you.

# Within These Four Walls

YOUR PATH

Upon looking at her path,
she was pleased with what she saw.
There were flowers along the edges,
the sun was tucked neatly behind the clouds;
for this was how she liked it.
As she started to make her way down it,
a new path appeared alongside her own.
It was fancier than hers:
smoother,
tidier,
neater.
And now when she looked upon her path
she saw the cracks,
the ridges,
and the bumps.
The feeling of pleasure now gone,
she grudgingly carried on walking down her path.
If only it were like that other path,
she thought,
I would be a lot happier.
Eventually, she decided to step away from her path
and onto the new, fancier one.
This is better she thought,
as she skipped down the new path.
But soon, the new path became weary.
The smooth surface made her slip,
there were no flowers on this path,
and the sun was too bright for her eyes.

## The Aftermath

Realising she missed her own path,
she stepped back across.
She still saw the cracks,
the ridges,
and the bumps,
but she didn't mind them as much now.
She liked the flowers
and the sun tucked behind the clouds.
My path may not be perfect,
she thought,
but it is mine.

MOVING FORWARD FROM HURT

When someone has hurt you, when you let a person in and they abuse that trust, it changes you. Moving forward, it becomes harder to open up to others because of what that person did to you. You start to question your judgement, doubt your heart – will the next person hurt me again? You start shutting down yourself to people because you are no longer sure who will stay and who will leave. The red flags you thought you could see become blurred. If you couldn't see it before, if you couldn't see the warning signs, how will you be able to see it now?

Maybe there was a warning, a red flag. Maybe that person said something to you, acted in a certain way, let you down more times than one, and you let it pass. You may regret that now because of what they did to you, but it is natural to want to see the best in someone. It is only natural to want to give things a chance and to let the little things slide. But now, looking back, you can see that those little things weren't little at all. They were all red flags, warnings, of the hurt that was about to come. But you can see this now, and you have learnt from this experience. You may still carry the hurt with you, but looking forward, you will be more alert and aware. While you cannot protect yourself completely, now you know what things you should watch out for, it will be easier.

But maybe there were no warning signs. Maybe there was nothing. Maybe looking back, you can't see anything. The hurt came completely out of the blue, and it left you stunned and shocked. It's so easy to start doubting your own abilities after this. To start questioning why you couldn't see it, or how you can possibly see it or prevent it in the future. But the truth is, sometimes people surprise us. We think we know who they are, but they turn out to be someone else entirely. But don't let this experience make you think the hurt happened because of you, because of something you did or didn't do. It was nothing to do with you – it was all to do with them.

Moving forward from this hurt and abuse of trust is so hard. How can you let someone else in when you know you're opening yourself up to the chance to be hurt again? How can you see love in the same light? Maybe you'll start to see love differently, through a harder, more clinical lens. Maybe you'll shut your heart off completely because you think that way you can never get hurt. But neither of these things will lead you anywhere good. Neither of these things will bring you happiness, peace or love.

Maybe you will see love in a different way, but perhaps it doesn't have to be in a bad way, just different. Maybe you'll simply tread more cautiously, aware of who should deserve your heart and who maybe doesn't. Maybe you'll be aware that some people aren't always

what they seem straight away and so you will allow
relationships time before you make that leap. But
perhaps all of this is a good thing. You're giving time
and consideration as to who you let in.

Whatever happens though, don't let the hurt that the
person caused you make you shut your heart off to the
world. There are so many people out there who will
love you deeply, who will gain your trust and never lose
it, who will stay and never leave. Finding these people
is worth the risk that comes with opening up your
heart. Finding these special people who will come into
your life and bring light, love and everything you've
wanted with them, is worthwhile. Keep your heart
open, but going forward, know it's okay if you do this
with caution.

Γ YOURSELF AS AN AFTERTHOUGHT

ɪ "no" to people.

It's okay to take a few days, weeks, or months away.

It's okay to heal in silence and solitude.

It's okay to take your time.

It's okay to focus on yourself.

It's okay to change your mind.

It's okay to cancel a friend last minute.

It's okay to ask for some space.

It's okay to not reply to that person who's bringing you down.

It's okay to not post on social media.

It's okay to have some "me" time.

It's okay to ask for help.

It's okay to let go of the feeling of obligation to respond to everyone who emails/texts/calls you.

And it's more than okay to put yourself, your health, and your wellbeing first.

OUTGROWN

There may be periods in your life when after a beautiful transformation, you no longer feel free in the spaces you used to go. The friends you once saw you can no longer connect with. This hometown feels like its holding you down rather than holding you up. The things you used to do no longer bring you joy. You feel enclosed and trapped.

But this is okay.

All that has happened is that you have simply outgrown who you used to be. Now you see the world in a different light you need to cut the strings that are tying you down.

You need to let go of what is making you shrink so you can be free once again to grow and breathe into this new you.

Transformations are beautiful, but you have to give this new you the space and environment it needs to grow and flourish; otherwise, you'll never feel free.

# The Aftermath

WHY I NEED TO BE BY MYSELF

I know if you were here
you'd make everything okay.
I know you would heal my wounds.
I know you would whisper away my sorrows with your
soothing words.
I know I'd feel safe in your arms like nothing could
ever harm me.
I know, with you, I would never feel alone.
But I also know this feeling would be temporary,
because every time you leave
I fall apart again.
I'm tired of always falling apart when you're not here.
I'm tired of only ever feeling okay in your presence.
I don't want to heal temporarily anymore,
I want to heal permanently.
I want to become the voice that can stitch myself back
together.
I want to feel enough when I'm in my own company.
I want to feel safe in my own arms.
I want to become whole again.
And I know to do this,
to heal and feel complete,
I need to be by myself.

# Within These Four Walls

## BE COMFORTABLE ON YOUR OWN FIRST

Until you can find peace and
solitude in your own company,
you can never know if you're
choosing to be with someone
out of love or loneliness.

✦

## THE KIND OF PEOPLE YOU NEVER FORGET

You gave me kindness when I
thought I deserved none.
No person like yourself can
ever be forgotten in a hurry.

✦

## HEARTBREAK

When your heart
breaks do not look
for another to fix it.

Look to yourself.

JUDGEMENT

How can you understand the decisions someone makes if you do not understand their story?

How can you change the way you see the world if you do not allow yourself to see it through another's eyes?

How can you feel compassion for someone if you do not first imagine what they are going through?

How can you pass judgement on someone when you cannot know exactly what's going through their mind or what brought them to this moment?

How can you know what you would do in their situation when you have never lived their life?

You should never judge someone before you know and completely understand their story, and seeing how none of us can ever truly understand another's story because of the impossibility to actually live their life, maybe it's easier if we all just stop judging one another altogether.

# Within These Four Walls

REWRITE YOUR STORY

She wanted a clean slate:
to start life again,
to leave the past behind her.
To throw out the old book
and grab a brand new one,
untainted from everything
that has already been.
If only she realised
right here,
in the present moment,
you have this chance
to start afresh.
Every day,
every hour,
every minute,
every second,
brings a brand-new moment
to use as you please.
Each moment is your
chance to rewrite
your story;
it is never too late
to start over.

# The Aftermath

UNWAVERING LOVE

I thought to be loved by someone I had to give them compromises and excuses for the way they sometimes treated me, as a thank you for being with me in the first place. I thought love was about being grateful for simply being viewed as 'wanted' in the first place when so many others turned away at the sight of my baggage. But now I realise this isn't love.

Love is not, I can treat you like this because you can't do that. Love is not, I will love you, but only under these circumstances and when it is convenient for me. Love is not, if I do this for you, you have to give me something in return.

Love is, being seen as yourself before any labels or baggage that weigh you down. Love is, never using those things against you. Love is, standing beside you and supporting you throughout the highs and lows.

Love is not about favours, compromises, or conditions. Love is whole, consistent, and unwavering.

Never let someone convince you otherwise because everyone deserves the unwavering kind of love.

# Within These Four Walls

## THE PAST IS THE PAST

"I don't understand," he said, "how can you still love
me after seeing the worst parts of me?"

She replied, "Because it is those parts of you that
make you the person you are today. And I love who
you are."

✦

## WHOLE

No matter how broken you feel
on the inside,
no one should ever be allowed
to treat you anything less than whole.

✦

## REMINDER

Stay true to yourself.
Stay true to who you are.
Stay true to those who
make you feel at home.

## WE ARE ALL THE SAME

Things every human being on the planet has in common:

- We all share and experience the same emotions of love, fear, joy, sadness, grief, anger, hurt, and compassion.
- We are all born the same way, and we all die the same way.
- We all share the same moon, sun, stars and sky.
- We all want to feel connected to someone or something.
- We all breathe the same air and walk on the same earth.
- We all have a body, a heart, and a mind.
- We all want to have somebody to love and to be loved in return.
- None of us want to suffer.
- We all need the same things to survive.
- We all just want to be happy.

If you remember this when you meet others, it is possible to connect with anyone and everyone you meet in life, because deep down, we are all the same.

UNCERTAIN

Life is filled
with far more uncertainties
than solid plans
and fixed futures.
And even those things
can crumble
in a moment
due to something unexpected
and unforeseen.
So be okay,
with not knowing everything.
Be okay,
with not knowing what lies ahead.
A future unknown
is a future
filled with possibilities.
You don't have to
always know the ending
or how you will get there,
to know it will
all work out
and be okay.

need a purpose
to feel, should be here on this earth.
You being here is purposeful enough.

You don't need a list of physical achievements
to prove you are worthy.
You are already worthy enough.

You don't need an agenda
to feel the day was successful and worthwhile.
Just to have gotten through the day, is enough.

You don't need to have done anything today,
except breathe and live,
moment to moment,
to realise you deserve to be here
just as much as anyone else.

THE GULF

When you finally feel you have
everything under control,
you've made peace with your situation,
you're grateful for this life
and everything you have,
you see something that triggers
a tsunami of emotions.
An airplane in the sky,
clothes you've never worn,
tickets from places you never made,
textbooks left unfinished;
all reminders of a life you lost.
They wedge open the splinter
inside your heart into a gulf of
mourning, grief, and loss.
It is impossible to close the gulf
back up as quickly as it was torn open.
You may find yourself trapped
in the gulf for days at a time,
with no view of escape.
But you will close it back up.
For every positive thought,
the gap becomes smaller.
So flood your mind
with thoughts of everything
you have gained in this new life:
lists of gratitude,
letting go of what could have been,

embracing this moment
with clarity and understanding.
While at the same time
giving yourself kindness and
compassion for this moment.
Sometimes it can take
just a few moments
to close the gulf back up,
other times it may take much longer.
But it will close back up,
and you will be okay once again.
Take heart,
you will be okay once again.

PURPOSE

Don't let other people's certainty about their life's purpose make you question your existence if you do not know yours. Some people will have big, loud, passionate purposes, while others may have smaller, quieter purposes that come and go and change day by day. It does not mean your life is, therefore, worth less than theirs or that people do not need you as much. Your life is just as important and valued, and there will always be room here for you too.

# The Aftermath

FEAR OF THINGS I USED TO DO SO EASILY

I know that when I leave this house, there will be fears for things I have never been afraid of before as it will all be so new and unfamiliar: meeting people I once knew, small talk in supermarkets, holding conversations at parties – things I did nearly every day for twenty years.

I won't laugh at myself for these seemingly insignificant fears that I once found so easy, for they are significant to me now, and that's all that matters. There is no shame in being afraid. I will embrace the fears as I face them, tackling each fear one at a time as I slowly readjust to everyday things I used to do.

It is normal to be afraid of things that have become so unfamiliar to you, no matter how much you have grown or how much time has passed.

But you will find,
maybe straight away,
or perhaps it will take a while;
that you will be okay,
and you will overcome
these fears someday,
one at a time.

PAPER ACHIEVEMENTS

Please do not decide
that you must already know me
based upon my age.
For I have already experienced things,
felt things,
gone through things,
most people only go through
over the course
of their entire life.
Please do not judge me
for the lack of countries I have seen,
the lack of qualifications I hold,
or the lack of social events I have been too.
Please do not look
at my list of achievements on paper
and assume
because it is blank
I have not experienced the world.
For there are far richer ways
to experience the world
than those you can put on paper.

# The Aftermath

BLOOM AND THEN ACCEPT NOTHING LESS

I take part of the responsibility
for how I let some people
treat me in the past.
I can see now,
in more ways than one,
I let it happen.
Because my self-worth
was planted so far underground,
buried in shame and loathing,
I didn't know when
someone was mistreating me,
as it was no different
to how I was treating myself.

But one day I decided
enough was enough.
I wanted,
needed,
to see the light again.
I started to sow light and love into myself
and ever so slowly,
inch by inch,
my self-worth grew.
Years have gone by
since that moment
I decided to change,
and I've reached heights
I once never thought were possible;

## Within These Four Walls

I have bloomed.

Now I know I will never
let anyone treat me badly again,
because I will accept nothing less
than what I give myself:

love
light
support
softness
kindness
gentleness.

HOLD YOURSELF HIGH

You will meet people who will choose not to understand your story or how far you have come. They will look at you, and they will look right through you, asking insignificant questions about yourself thinking that is the best way to get to know who you are. They will ask where you are from, what your job is, where you have studied. Things that maybe you hold little or no answers for. You will be left standing there feeling unsure about yourself and maybe thinking there is not enough to you.

But there is enough to you; they just chose to ask you the wrong questions. If they had asked you: What have you been through to reach this moment? What is it that makes you stand so tall today? What moves your soul and makes you who you are? Maybe then you would feel confident about who you are today and hold pride in how far you have come. Maybe then you would answer those questions exhaling with the breath of belief of how much you have achieved.

So when they choose to look through you – leaving awkward pauses when your achievements are not up to their standards as you see the judgement fall on their face – I hope you remember to stand there thinking about all the things they don't know, bringing light to the parts of you that would make them tremble in awe.

You do not need to stand in their presence and prove you are worthy to them. You just need to hold yourself high, never losing sight of all the things you have overcome to reach this moment, and never forgetting just how much you have achieved.

# A Conversation with

# Wisdom

ANNIVERSARIES

Today is not a day
to mourn
all I have lost.
Today is a day
to celebrate
all I have gained.

# A Conversation with Wisdom

Wisdom pulled up a chair beside my bed and said, "Okay, let's do this. Tell me everything you have learnt in these past six months."

"It's strange," I said to Wisdom, "how you can go through life thinking and trying to convince yourself you're happy, for years on end, and then only when you finally get a taste of what real happiness is, do you suddenly realise just how much you've been missing out on all this time.

I think I'm starting to realise that I wasn't truly happy before all this, and maybe I hadn't been for a very long time. The happiness I felt before was the fleeting kind. It was through things I touched (objects, people, achievements), rather than through things I felt (gratitude, peace, calm, contentment). The happiness I have now is more deep-rooted and steadier than I've ever had before. I know this is because I'm learning that my happiness is dependent on things from within, rather than external factors.

These past months have been the wakeup call I needed but was always too afraid to follow. By having my life simplified and being forced to take a massive step back, everything has been put into perspective. These six months have magnified my gratitude towards so many things – things I didn't even know I could and should

120

be grateful for! I'm so grateful for having a garden and being able to spend time outside. I'm so grateful I still have the use of my legs to be able to walk outside and around the house. I'm so grateful for my family who make me laugh daily and who couldn't be more perfect. I'm so grateful for my group of friends who are so understanding and supportive towards my situation and have been so kind in sending me messages and cards when I can't see them. I'm so grateful for my dog and her unconditional love and company. I'm so grateful for being able to write my blog and connect with so many people online. The list of gratitude is truly endless.

When I am well enough to leave the house, see my friends, go for walks, I now know just how much better those experiences will be for me because I'll appreciate them so much more. Leaving the house is something 99% of people do daily, but does anyone ever stop to think just how amazing it is that they can do that? Just think how lucky you are! The thing is you never know what will happen in life, so it's important to make the most of everything you have while you still have it, and to never take anything for granted."

# A Conversation with Wisdom

"I see we're still here," Wisdom said, looking around my house that I've come to know like the back of my hand. "Well, you must have learnt a lot from this past year." Wisdom took its seat and said in earnest, "Please, tell me all about it."

So I told Wisdom, "I guess I never comprehended just how much there was to learn about myself and the world. I thought those first six months provided me with enough growth and knowledge to go ahead and fully live my life, thinking I had learnt all there was to learn. But I didn't even scratch the surface. It seems the more you think you know, the more you realise you don't. However, I do know that I have learnt and grown more in this past year than my twenty years previously.

For the longest time, I tried to run away from my thoughts. I thought that if I kept running for long enough and distanced myself from what was happening within, they would just go away. But of course, it isn't that simple. Your thoughts won't go away, and you can't outrun them forever. A day will come when you realise this, and you conclude it's better to turn around and face them. This is what becoming housebound did to me: it forced me to stop and face what I had been running from.

I was lucky that just before becoming housebound, I had started a meditation class that completely changed my life. The reason for this was because when I was finally forced to be alone with my thoughts, meditation and mindfulness gave me the tools I needed. They allowed me to practise giving my thoughts and emotions the space to breathe and to observe them from a distance, without judgement. This way, I could see them clearly for what they were, rather than when I was up close and projecting my fear and worry onto them, which always distorts them.

It was through this non-judgemental space that I could see that my thoughts were just that, thoughts. And for the most part, my thoughts weren't even a running dialogue of what was happening in front of me, but a continuous loop of things that have happened or could happen. And that was a revelation for me; to realise I was pretty much always thinking about things that weren't fact or actuality, and that I was rarely just living in the moment with what was in front of me.

In this new space of awareness, I could also notice just how often different emotions would come and go. It was like my mind was a hotel, and my emotions were guests; I couldn't control when they arrived, and I couldn't control when they left, but I could control which ones I took notice of and talked to. This awareness of the fact my emotions were always temporary allowed me to stop being so caught up in them, especially the negative ones. So when they did arise, I could watch them from a distance and recognise that they'll pass again soon.

I really am so immensely grateful that these 365 days have happened to me because they have been the perfect opportunity for me to practise and finally learn all this. It's hard to say if I would have done so otherwise, as nothing forces you to stop or be alone with your thoughts quite like a year of being housebound does!!"

PERSPECTIVE

I told Wisdom, "Someone recently said to me they felt sad and angry on my behalf because of my situation and the fact I'm still so ill."

"Well," Wisdom replied, "what did you say to them when they said that?"

"My automatic response to them was, "Please do not feel sorry for me that I am still so ill. I may not be able to do much, but I am still happy and peaceful. If you want to feel sorry for anyone, feel sorry for those who have it all and still cannot be happy. As people often say, life is sometimes 10% what happens to you and 90% how you react to it.

You may see a girl who is housebound, but I feel like a girl who is incredibly lucky not to be bedbound. You may see a girl who should be angry at her situation and at the doctors who can't help, but I feel like a girl who can never see the point or purpose in anger. You may see a girl who doesn't get to see her friends, but I feel like a girl who is so immensely grateful for the friends I have knowing they'll always wait for me. You may see a girl with little chance of recovery having been ill a long time, but I feel like a girl who has complete trust that I will one day get better. You may see a girl who should be out partying and living life like other 21-year olds, but I feel like a girl who has gained so much more than any 20 something experience could have taught me. You may see a girl who should be unhappy in life, but I feel like a girl who wakes up every day and can't see a reason why I shouldn't and can't be happy."

As they say, sometimes it's all about perspective."

# Within These Four Walls

AT TWO YEARS HOUSEBOUND

Curled up in the chair so familiar Wisdom had none of the sadness or disbelief that was reflected in my own pained face. Wisdom said cheerily, "So, here we go again, are you ready?"

"I don't want to do this again," I told Wisdom, "I'm not sure I can keep doing this."

"You don't have to talk to me, you know, the choice is yours."

Thinking about the person I would be today or the life I would be living if these past two years hadn't happened to me, I realised I never wanted to imagine it and felt overwhelming gratitude that they had. Taking a deep breath, I said, "Okay, I'm ready."

"Then let's begin."

"I remember when I first hit six months of being housebound, I swore I would not allow it to become one year. That would be way too surreal. The idea of being housebound for an entire year was simply unfathomable. When it became one year, I told myself it simply could not turn to two years. Nope. No way. I could not handle that. That was more than I could bear. But of course, here I am, two years housebound, and getting through all the days I once thought I wouldn't cope with."

If you're reading this you may be thinking there's no way I could handle being completely housebound for two years – I just couldn't do it. And yet you could. Luckily, I hope you don't have to! But if it came to it, you could manage it because us humans can endure so much more than we think. We think we can't do things. We think we can't handle it. We think it's too much for us to cope with. And yet we do cope. Even when we don't have a choice in the matter (like being housebound). Even though at times, it can be so difficult. We still cope. Every. Single. Time. Because we're all still here, all still getting through 100% of the days we think we can't handle.

When we stop and think about it, many of us are surprised at how much we can and have endured. I know I am. I keep getting surprised at all the little and big things I tell myself I can't cope with – self-injections, three-day migraines, not leaving the house once in 2018 – and yet I do.

So if there's something in your life right now that you think you won't be able to cope with, know you've coped with every single day so far in your life, so the likelihood is you'll be okay in the end.

# Within These Four Walls

"I remember the day as clear as anything," I said, showing Wisdom the photo of me in London that captured the very day I contracted glandular fever, exactly six years ago to this date. "I had just turned sixteen, having finished a very intense week of GCSE mock exams, I was in London with my parents visiting my sister who was working there on her placement year from university. Enjoying the luxuries of London, me and my sister went sightseeing, visited Portobello market, had afternoon tea, bought red velvet cupcakes at the famous Hummingbird bakery, and celebrated Chinese New Year in Times Square.

Walking towards the restaurant on our last day, I suddenly started to feel I was coming down with something. By the time we got home, it was clear I'd picked up the flu. What none of us knew at the time and wouldn't know for another six months was that on that cold, wet, winter's day in London, I had actually contracted glandular fever, and whether I knew it or not, on Sunday 10th February 2013, my life had completely changed.

I never recovered from glandular fever, and two years later I finally got diagnosed with M.E. What makes me feel sad though is the fact that girl in the picture didn't know the rest of the story. But I don't mean that as a, "she had no idea what was about to come", I actually mean I feel sad she didn't know about the part when things were going to be okay.

The part where she would achieve happiness in a place least expected. The part where she would learn to practise self-compassion instead of self-criticism. The part where she would learn that although her journey is different from everyone else's and not the one she had in mind, it doesn't make it worse, it just makes it different. The part where she would learn her self-worth is more than achievements on paper. The part where she would learn to let go of her perfectionism and be happy with who she is. The part where she would learn to make peace with her illness. The part where she would learn to accept her life for what it was and be okay with that.

I wish I could have gotten the chance to tell her all that. I wish I could have told her that things turned out more than okay. The fact that I grieve for the girl in the photo more than the present me who is now entering the third year of being housebound maybe says it all. Because the truth is, it really is more than okay."

USING YOUR ENERGY FOR GOOD THINGS ONLY

"I've come to see energy as a gift", I said, turning to Wisdom.

"What do you mean?" Wisdom replied.

"Well," I explained, "before I fell ill, I remember how I used to waste my energy on a lot of things I didn't enjoy doing. I was applying to do a degree in a subject I knew I wouldn't like, but I felt a degree was better than no degree. I went to parties with people I felt I couldn't be myself with therefore I couldn't enjoy but still went as I didn't want to "miss out". I did activities through feeling obligated to do them rather than asking myself would I benefit from this.

But since falling ill, my outlook on this subject is something that has changed dramatically. Having limited energy means you only have a few activities you can do each day as you do not have enough energy to do everything. Although this can be frustrating, it does mean you always end up prioritising what things are most important to you and what activities you enjoy the most.

I would never now choose to do something I didn't enjoy, but why did I do this when I had full energy levels? Why do so many of us still put so much energy into things we know won't benefit us? The reason why my perspective has shifted so much on this subject is that, as I said, I've come to see energy as a gift. If someone handed it to me right now, I would do everything I could to make sure I used this gift for good things only. I would never waste it on anything or anyone that brought me down rather than up. I would never waste it on something not worth my time. I would cradle it with my whole being and nurture it the best I could.

I think the best way to always make sure you use your energy for good is to ask yourself, "Is what I'm about to do going to make me happy or benefit myself or others in some way?" Putting a label on your energy levels saying "treat with care" will help remind you to always think about what you're putting your energy into. Your energy is too precious to be spent on things that don't bring you happiness. And if you are someone who has full energy levels every day, try to remember what an incredible privilege this is and how many people would love to have this gift."

# Within These Four Walls

"So clearly the universe thought you had more to learn," Wisdom chuckled while exploring the four by five-meter extent of my world.

I couldn't help but laugh at the joke. "Yes, clearly," I replied, "although I'm not entirely sure what it is I have left to learn."

"There is always more one can learn."

"Of course you would say that! But yes, I guess I do realise that now."

"You seem okay about today," Wisdom asked curiously, "I didn't think you would be in all honesty."

"No, neither did I," I replied, "but I realise now that the future always seems scarier when it's in my mind than when it becomes my reality. I've often told people how I never resent being housebound because I'm always just so grateful that I'm not bedbound as I sadly know of too many people who are with these illnesses.

Underneath that statement though was a silent panic questioning how I would ever cope if I did become bedbound, but the idea of that was too scary even to contemplate, so I always pushed it away. But a few months ago, after suffering from a crash, I became what I always feared: bedbound. The strange thing about the experience though is that it wasn't the overwhelming panic I thought I would experience when this fear came true. I didn't think much about it. Instead, it was just, happening.

I think the reason for this is because fear doesn't really live in the present moment with you; it's always the unknown and possibilities that are scary. My mind adapted to the new surroundings so quickly that I didn't really register it until afterwards. The things I became grateful for got even smaller as my physical world decreased once again. I started to dream for all the things I had only a month or two ago. Of course, the sadness and heartbreak joined me into this new phase, but the fear moved on. It found new things for me to be afraid of: the fear of never getting better, the fear of only going downhill from here. But the original fear of being bedbound left.

I think there's a big lesson to learn here, and that is, things change. Circumstances change. And our fears continuously change. By realising that our fears are not 'fixed' objects, it can help us to step back from them and see them as nothing more than imaginations of the mind, rather than facts. We can accept they will always be there, and yes, they may or may not come true, but we don't have to allow them to overwhelm or terrify us. By remembering that the fears we currently have are only temporary and will one day move on, it can release the power they hold over us, and therefore enable us to be able to let them go.

Although I do not know why no matter what I do, I can't seem to get better, I do know that this is not forever. I know that even when everything still seems to be going wrong, that doesn't mean you should ever stop doing right. And I know that there will come a day sometime in the future when I look back on this period of time and wonder how on earth I got through it the way I have."

# A Conversation with Wisdom

BAD MOMENTS ARE A PART OF OUR JOURNEY

"How have you been holding up?" Wisdom asked, knowing that this year has been hard for me as my health still fails to show any signs of improvement.

I responded, "This year has been such a mixed bag of emotions. There have been so many days of peace, happiness, and contentment. But there have also been the moments of heartbreak, frustration, and sadness. But that's okay. It's always okay. This idea some of us have that we shouldn't feel pain or sadness is not right. The more we try and resist these moments or emotions, the longer they stay. By embracing the good times as well as the bad, we live life in constant acceptance. It allows us to move through life without clinging to anything and to just be at one with the moment and the roller coaster that is life.

My moments of heartbreak, frustration, and sadness never seem significant to me, and I can often forget I have them, simply because they pass so quickly as I've learnt never to resist them. I can recognise now that negative emotions are a part of me and my journey. They're never going to leave me, ever. And again, that's okay. Emotions are just emotions. They come, and they go. We don't need to get wrapped up in them. We don't need to cling to them. We just need to accept them for what they are, embrace them with kindness and compassion, and stay calm as we watch them pass.

The earlier we can accept these bad moments are going to be with us for life, the quicker they pass, and the sooner we can be at peace once again."

# A Conversation with Wisdom

"Okay," Wisdom said softly, "give me your all and give it to me honestly."

I answered, "I do not know what life is like as a twenty-something-year-old outside these four walls I call my home. It's so so surreal, especially when I write it down or say it out loud to other people, but the thing is I don't know any different. When I first became housebound, I remember I was always counting the days. "It's been X days since I left the house, it's now been Y days..." But I realised the counting this year has stopped. I don't know why. Maybe it's because it has been so long now it hurts a little bit to think about it too much. Or maybe I'm just so focused on keeping my hope and trust alive that these housebound days will very soon be over that I don't like to dwell on it.

The thing is when it comes to "time" we often measure it wrong. If I got offered the chance to give three years of my life in exchange for a lifetime's worth of knowledge, growth, wisdom, and happiness, I would take it. This is how I am starting to view my time being housebound: a few years of solitude and simplicity in exchange for the rest of my life to then be deep and meaningful.

I know how lucky I am to have gained the kind of insight I have at such a young age. Most people don't experience this kind of shift in perspective until much, much later in life, and so to have this chance and opportunity to learn all these lessons so young really is a gift. I truly am grateful for these years, and I wouldn't give them back even if I could.

Although my situation sounds terrible, I hold so much peace and happiness here in these four walls; the bad moments are very far and few, and I want to make sure I always remember that. I know in the future I won't look back on this period of time with sadness, but with an understanding that I wouldn't be the person I am today, if I hadn't had gone through all this first."

# Part Three:

# The Calm

# Within These Four Walls

IT DOESN'T HAVE TO BE A BAD DAY, IT CA
BAD MOMENT

Realistically, no day is 100% good or 100% bad. Instead, it is a blend of both good and bad moments. Some days the good outweighs the bad, and others the bad outweighs the good.

But that doesn't have to make it a good or bad day, it just makes the day a combination of both good and bad moments.

The reason why it's essential to learn the difference is because life is experienced in moments, not days.

If you say the day is bad, you have to wait a whole twenty-four hours for the next chance at having a good day.

But if you say it is a bad moment, then you have the opportunity right there and then to make the next moment a good one.

So always remember, it doesn't have to be a bad day, it can just be a bad moment.

# The Calm

Wisdom laid three choices in front of her: the past, the present, and the future. Wisdom turned to her and said, "Choose one, for you can only choose one because none can be together at the same time."

She turned to the past and asked, "What do you offer me?" The past answered, "I can relay for you the best and worst moments of your life. I can allow you to see where you've gone wrong and where you've gone right. I can be the cause of your darkest moods or the keeper of your best memories."

Next, she turned to the future and asked, "What do you offer me?" The future answered, "I do not yet exist, you may do with me as you please. I can be the cause of your deepest anxiety or the visions you wish to dream upon."

Lastly, she turned to the present and asked, "What do you offer me?" The present answered simply, "I can let you live."

## CALM AT THE BOTTOM OF THE OCEAN

Through this mess, there is calm.
Delve deep, and you will find it.
Look too hard though,
and you will lose it.
For the calmness does not
need to be searched,
only found,
for it is already within you
and always has been.
Like the sand at the bottom of the ocean
it will always be there,
silent and unmoving.
No matter how hard
the waves crash on the surface,
or how busy the ocean gets,
you will still find calm
upon the ocean floor.
If only one could always
remember its presence
the world would be
a much happier place.
But for now,
this ocean is yours,
so sink to the bottom
and be still once again.

# The Calm

When something happens to you that causes your life to turn 180 degrees, the transition period between your old life which is no longer viable, and the new one you've been landed with can be a tough journey. At first, this new life seems scary and full of the unknown. You spend your time wishing you had your old life back, wishing the thing that happened to you didn't happen. You struggle to work out how to live this new life.

But after a while, you come to realise maybe this new life isn't as bad as it initially seemed, maybe it's even better than the life you thought you had planned. You slowly start to notice the little joys in life again. You begin to feel a deep sense of gratitude for things you didn't know you could feel. You learn that the small things in life really are the big things. Thoughts that would have once preoccupied your mind in your old life now seem so trivial in this new one. You start to feel a glimmer of hope that maybe things will be okay after all. You become brave enough to open the door to this new life and embrace this new way of living.

Although you may have many times where you still doubt this new life, these moments become more and more fleeting. After a while, you start to realise maybe this was the life you were meant to live all along. Maybe this was the path you were meant to take. You mentally list all the lessons and experiences you wouldn't have learnt if you hadn't had this new life. You look back and imagine what your life could have been if the thing had never happened, and you thank the universe it did. You become grateful for everything that's happened, and you wouldn't go back and change it even if you could. Because sometimes, when it feels like things are falling apart, you realise they are actually falling into place.

CONVERSATIONS

To the person who said to me, "I wish for your better health so you can live your life again" – I want you to know that my life has not stopped. I am still here. I am still living. It may have taken a different turn, but that does not mean my life has been paused or put on hold. My life is as real, and as present as anyone else's, it's just different, that's all.

To the person who said to me, "I can't imagine what you're going through" – while I appreciate you acknowledging the hardship I have to face, through these words you are separating my life from your own. You are placing me in a box and labelling my life as "too hard to understand". Instead, maybe you could take the time to try and imagine what I'm going through. To step closer to me instead of stepping away. To listen and attempt to understand, even if it is difficult or uncomfortable for you.

To the person who said to me, "I could never do what you do" – you don't know that. You don't know what you can or can't do until you are tested with it. And you'll find if that day comes, you survive; each day you get through, you always persevere.

# Within These Four Walls

YOU WILL FIGURE IT OUT AS YOU GO ALONG

You don't need to have
everything figured out
to know you'll be okay.
There is a beauty
and rawness
in the unknown,
the open road,
the uncertain:
where anything is possible.
There is little room
for growth
in set destinations,
so take heart
that the unknown
is the best place for you.
You will figure it out
as you go along,
one moment at a time.

# The Calm

TRUSTING IN THE UNKNOWN

Something I get asked so often is how do I trust so blindly in my journey and in knowing I will get better? My answer is always because I choose to. I choose to trust. I choose to put my complete faith in the unknown. I choose to believe that in order to bloom, you need to be planted first. I choose to remember that good things always take time. I choose to have absolute confidence that one day, all this effort I'm putting into getting better will eventually pay off.

It can be so scary to do this. To reach out and trust in something when you have nothing to grasp or hold on to. But I've noticed in the past that when I've allowed myself to trust in the journey's I cannot yet foresee, they have often ended up being the exact paths I needed to take.

The flip side of all of this is not trusting. Not trusting that things will get better. Not trusting that everything will work out. And feeling like that is really upsetting and hard. So, the choice is yours; you can doubt everything that is happening to you, or you can give yourself permission to trust in all the things you cannot yet see.

DON'T LOOK BACK

It is both
scary and exhilarating
when you realise
you can no longer
be who you used to be
or go back to living the life you used to
because you have grown
to the point
of no return.

Although this thought may
terrify you,
don't try and resist the
growth or fit back into
your old life.
You will never be happy again
in a place that is no longer
meant for you.

Let this growth take you
into the unknown.
Step into the wilderness
and don't look back,
for there is magic
to be found here.

# The Calm

WILDERNESS

Here in the wilderness, she stood.
Barefoot, courage dripping from
her bones – with nothing but the
wind to guide her, she found the
strength to trust and let go.

# Within These Four Walls

A LETTER TO MY FUTURE SELF

Dear Evie,

I'm writing you this letter for the future because I want you to remember this moment.

Right now, you are lying in the garden staring at the beautiful summer sky.

You're happy, you're content, but you can hear the chatter and laughter of friends and family from nearby gardens, and it reminds you how much you miss your own family and friends.

You don't have the energy to see them right now, and you haven't for a long while, and this makes you feel sad.

You never considered seeing your friends and family as something that one day you wouldn't be able to do. You never knew that this thing you used to take for granted would be taken away from you.

You never saw it as something to be grateful for and appreciate.

So I'm here to remind you not to make the same mistake twice.

I'm also writing this letter to you because while travelling the world, meeting new people, and experiencing new things is something you constantly dream of and desire, if you had to pick one thing you could do right now, you really just want to spend the time with the people you love.

# The Calm

To be able to visit your brother and sister and see their hometowns, to see your grandparents and spend time with them, to chat endlessly to your best friend and go on adventures together blaring Hamilton out the car, to sit around the table for a family meal and to be together during holidays and birthdays, to have dinner parties and picnics with your girl group and join them on holiday.

This is what you want right now more than anything. I want you to remember this, because while big adventures are amazing, and going off and catching up on your 20s is at the top of your list for things to do when you are better, as tempting as it may be to just get on the first plane out of here, if you were to fall ill again, or something happened to you, and this was all you chose to do, you would regret it immensely.

Please don't ever take being with loved ones for granted again.

Right now you miss them more than anything, so if in a few years you're trying to figure out where to prioritise your energy and time, I hope this will help give you your answer.

Love E xx

# Within These Four Walls

## BALANCE

How incredible is it that you have learnt the art of
balancing being patient for a future that is brighter,
whilst still fully living your life today.

✦

## HESITANT

Sometimes we just have to step forward with
an open heart, curiosity, and courage,
and find out where this path will take us.

✦

## GLOWING

Despite being buried here
in the wilderness of your
unknowns and darkness,
look at how beautifully
you are choosing
to grow,
to learn,
to let go.

You are glowing from this.

# The Calm

UNDERSTANDING THE BALANCE

Be soft they said,
but not so soft that you can't stay afloat through it all.

Be still they said,
but not so still that you forget the mountains you can move.

Be kind they said,
but not so kind that you forget your boundaries.

Be strong they said,
but not so strong that you can't let your walls come down.

Be quiet they said,
but not so quiet that you forget the power of your voice.

Be compassionate they said,
but not so compassionate that you forget to feed your own soul.

Be gentle they said,
but not so gentle that you forget to stand up for what's right.

SAYINGS

They say "everything happens for a reason" – but what about the people taken from life too young, or the disasters that leave nothing but devastation in its wake. Do these things also happen for a reason?

They say "you are only given what you can handle" – and yet how many people are crushed under the weight of their life, unable to cope. Is it okay to tell them they can handle it?

They say "everyone in life has a purpose" – but what about all those who can find no purpose, no one true calling. Are they therefore viewed as living less meaningful lives?

Maybe no saying can ever be universal. Maybe no one can apply a line or belief that fits so well into their own life into another's. Maybe we need to realise the words we counsel others with – however well-intentioned – might not have the same positive impact it had on our self. Perhaps it's time we start recognising that because everyone is different, no guidance can be the same.

# The Calm

SHINE

Don't let other people's success make you
think you are therefore failing in some way.
They are not succeeding ahead of you
or taking away your ability to succeed in the future,
they are simply shining right now
because this is their time to do so.
Be happy for them and know that one day
you too will have your moment to shine.

NEW YEAR'S REMINDERS

- If your year doesn't start off as you had planned, remember it isn't your only opportunity for a new beginning. Every day, every hour, every minute, every second, brings you a brand-new moment for you to breathe and start again.
- Your self-worth is not measured by your productivity.
- The future is not in your control.
- It's okay not to have any plans or goals because sometimes letting go and just going with the flow can be the best way to live.
- Don't try and attempt to solve your entire life in one instance; life unfolds only in moments, so it's much better just to focus your energy on one moment at a time.
- You can achieve far more in a year than you can in a month. And further still, you can achieve far more in two years than you can in just one.
- Try to let go of what you think your life should look like and instead just live life as it's happening.
- Always be kind to yourself. Always be kind to others.
- And finally remember: you are only alive in this moment. If you live your life continually planning for the future, you will miss out on all the moments that are taking place right now. So this moment is the best time to just live.

# The Calm

CHOOSE YOUR WORDS CAREFULLY

Every time I read your words,
they find their way into my heart.
Seeping through the cracks,
they echo in my body until
my beating heart has heard them.
Your words and my heart are now one;
connected and intertwined.
What magical powers you have,
that your words can do something so powerful
as to engrave them on my heart.
Thank you for sharing them with me.
With this understanding,
I will always make sure the words I write for others,
I write with the knowledge of the potential they have
to wrap themselves around another's heart,
like your words have with mine.

SOULMATE

He asked, "Do you believe in soulmates?"

She replied, "I believe there are some people in the world who are so brilliant for each other it just makes sense. When people see them together, they just fit. But these people are very rare and so lucky. I also don't think soulmate should be tied only to romantic love because you might find your soulmate in your best friend.

But I am cautious about the word soulmate because if you don't believe you have found your soulmate, then it can often feel like something is missing. Or even worse, say you think you have found your soulmate, and then something happens to them, or they leave your life, you may then lead yourself to believe you can never love again or ever feel that deeply connected to a person.

There is too much comparison when it comes to love, which doesn't make much sense because everyone is unique and therefore, will always make you feel slightly different. You can't repeat the exact same emotion; you can't repeat the exact same love. So say someone has left your life who you loved deeply, it's important to not then go out and try and replicate that exact kind of love with another because you won't find it again.

But that doesn't mean you can't find love again or feel connected to someone, it just means it's going to be different. But that's okay, different doesn't mean it's worse, it's just different. And this new person you find will bring you a new way to love and be loved."

## LOVE WITHOUT AN AGENDA

Do not judge those
who cannot be kind
if they have not been
shown kindness themselves.
For how can you be kind
if you do not know how?
Instead,
feel compassion for them
that they have never had the pleasure
to experience this emotion.
Show them all that they missed,
and hope it is not too late.

FORGIVENESS

You can forgive someone for the hurt they inflicted upon you, but not forget the pain they caused you. You can forgive someone and let them go, but not allowing the letting go to say that what they did to you was okay. You can forgive someone and wish them happiness, but also want nothing to do with them again.

Forgiveness is not about forgetting, reconciliation, or justifying their actions. Forgiveness does not require you to tell that person you've forgiven them or to let them back into your life. Forgiveness is something you do for you: for your soul, for your peace. It's about recognising that by holding onto the pain, the only person still being inflicted by the damage is you. You might hold onto the pain as you think it will make them realise what they have done – to hope they will finally see the hurt they have caused you. But the likelihood is if they caused you to hurt in the first place, they wouldn't recognise they're still hurting you now.

So let the hurt go. Let the pain and anger go. You are not doing this for them; you are doing this for you. You are doing this so you can live, so you can let go and move on. Forgiveness may feel like a weak thing to do, but it is through wisdom and knowledge that helps you recognise why forgiveness is so crucial for your happiness.

Don't wait for that person to acknowledge your pain. Don't wait for closure. Don't wait for them to see they hurt you. You may never get closure, and even if you do, it often doesn't do as much for you as you think. That's because the healing starts from within you, not from them. You have to make the conscious decision to let the hurt go. You have to decide to move on.

Forgiveness is one of the hardest things to do, especially when your pain isn't acknowledged or seen. But always remember, you are doing this for you. You are doing this because you deserve peace. You are doing this because you deserve a life free from hurt and pain. Don't let what they did to you take away your ability to feel peace because by doing that you are only allowing them to maximise the pain they have caused you. Don't let them have control over you anymore. Don't let them decide how you get to feel each day. Give up the pain and let it go. Let it go so you can live free from them and find peace in your life once again. You deserve that, especially after everything you have been through. You deserve a life filled with peace.

# The Calm

ANGER

"What do you do for me?" she asked.

Anger answered, "I block you from your path to peace and happiness. I distort your thoughts and emotions. I make you say things you regret after. I will hurt the people you love. I will hurt yourself. I will blame everything and everyone around me for the way I feel."

"Then why do you exist?" she asked, confused. "If you only bring misery into my life, what is your purpose?"

"I test your strength", Anger replied. "I am one of the strongest emotions you can feel. It takes great power to hold me in, to calm the fire before the storm, to recognise when I am on my way before I fully arrive. If you can overcome me, that shows you are by far stronger than all those who let me fly."

"How can I overcome you then?"

"By giving me the opposite of what I give you: compassion, patience, understanding, tolerance, calm. Feed me those things, and I cannot exist."

# Within These Four Walls

ADMIT WHEN YOU'RE IN THE WRONG

The person who confesses
they were in the wrong
makes one mistake.

The person who hides
they were in the wrong
makes two mistakes.

Only the wise can see this difference.

Have the courage
to acknowledge and admit
when you are
in the wrong,
and be open to
accepting you are
not always right.

This is how you
learn and grow
as a person.

# The Calm

RED LIGHT

Growth is knowing
the thoughts you have
in the red light of anger,
in the middle of the night,
in the middle of a storm,
are not accurate descriptions
of your true reality,
but heightened emotions
and fabricated thoughts.

Growth is acknowledging these thoughts,
but not involving yourself in them
as you see the false light
they are portrayed in.
Not reacting to them,
but allowing them to run
their course as you calmly
wait for them to pass.

WHEN I AM CALM...

I am aware.
I am mindful.
I am productive.
I am at my most powerful.
I am at my most beautiful.
I allow thoughts to come and go.
I positively affect those around me.
I make the best and wisest decisions.
I take my time responding to situations.
I do not let external circumstances affect me.
I live in the absence of stress, anger and negativity.
I contribute to the healing and peace of this world.
I don't let other people's attitude or energy disrupt me.
I do not get caught up in the storms of strong emotion.

# The Calm

## THE LITTLE THINGS

Sometimes the best moments in life
are not the parties
that leave you dancing until three am,
the spontaneous adventures,
or the late-night campfires.
Sometimes the best moments
are the little ones
in between all that:
a cuddle with your dog,
your morning cup of tea,
witnessing a beautiful sunset,
curling up on the sofa with a book,
sitting in the garden with your family,
driving with the windows down and music blaring.

Don't put all your expectations
into thinking that the 'big' times
should be what life is about.
Show up for the seemingly vanilla
and unremarkable moments,
and realise there is so much
happiness and joy
to be found in these moments too,
and just because they are smaller,
does not mean they hold any less joy.

LESSONS FROM NATURE

If you want to learn about life, look to nature:

The trees teach you that if you plant your roots deep enough, and give your growth enough time and patience, then you will stay grounded even throughout the storms. The flowers teach you that everyone's growth looks different; it's okay to grow at your own pace, and everything will bloom when it is ready. The wildflowers teach you to trust in letting go, as that is how you get planted, and to grow wherever you land.

The ocean teaches you that no matter how busy the ocean gets or how hard the waves crash on the surface, there is always calm upon the ocean floor. The mountains teach you that great things take time. The valleys teach you that even at the bottom, there is still beauty and peace to be found. The rivers teach you the importance of going with the flow.

The sky teaches you that no matter how many clouds there are or how dark it gets; the clouds will always pass and the blue sky is always there. The sun teaches you the elegance of consistency and to rise each morning no matter what happens or who is watching. The moon teaches you not to fear the darkness, and that even when you find yourself somewhere you do not seem to belong, shine so bright that no one will ever question your presence. The stars teach you that even in the darkness, there is still beauty to be uncovered here.

Spring teaches you the importance of nurturing yourself in order to grow. Summer teaches you about the joy of living in the moment. Autumn teaches you about letting go of the things that no longer serve you. Winter teaches you about the importance of rest and slowing down. All the seasons together teach you that even during the darkest of times, you are still growing and changing each day, that nothing can bloom all year round, and everything is always temporary.

# Within These Four Walls

ABOVE UNDERSTANDING AND REASON

You are allowed to trust
in all the things you cannot yet see.
You are allowed to find peace,
even amongst the things you cannot understand.
You are allowed to feel hope
with no reason or evidence as to why,
but just because you choose to.
You are allowed to experience moments of joy,
even when nothing is certain
and the darkness is everywhere.
You are allowed to be content,
even when this is not the place
you would choose to be.
You are allowed to be happy,
even if others cannot understand
or see that it is possible.
You are allowed to believe,
even against all the odds.
You are allowed to love your life,
even if it's not the life you envisioned or planned.

You are allowed to do all of these things and give no
reason or explanation why but just because you choose
to. And you are allowed to choose to feel and
experience all of these things, above understanding
and reason.

# The Calm

There is often
no rhyme or reason as to why
life can take unexpected turns.
But to question these turns is to resist,
and to resist,
is to lose oneself of peace.
No matter how unexpected the turn,
do not waste valuable energy wondering why,
for your peace should be treasured above all else
and sacrificed for nothing.
You are here,
and whether you like it or not,
that is that.
This unexpected turn
is not the end of your road,
it is so far from it.
There is so much more to come,
so many more stories to be written,
so much path up ahead.
So be at peace with this unexpected turn;
breathe into this moment of change,
and release your resistance as you go,
as before you know it
you'll be turning once again.

THE INVISIBLE RACE

"What's the rush?" Peace asked.

"There's just so much to do and so little time!" Stress replied anxiously.

"Let me rephrase my question," Peace replied. "What are you rushing for?"

Stress stopped and looked at Peace puzzled, "What do you mean, what am I rushing for?"

"Well," Peace said, "whatever you're rushing for must be important enough to sacrifice your inner peace and happiness for it, as that is exactly what you are doing. But then again, I struggle to understand what can possibly be more important in life than those things. It seems like everybody has decided that to look busy is better than to look idle; therefore, we must be busy all the time! But I think we've all forgotten why we feel the need to always be so busy.

It's like we are all participating in an invisible race, and yet there is no finish line, and there certainly is no prize. All I am suggesting is that the next time you feel stressed, maybe ask yourself, is what I am about to do worth sacrificing my inner peace and happiness for? If it's not, then you need to think about how you're going to prioritise those things and figure out a way to work around it."

# Within These Four Walls

## THE ART OF SLOWING DOWN

Why do we put so much
emphasis on moving forward?
When sometimes so much
more can be learnt from standing still.

✦

## GROWTH

You know you have come so far
when other people's
energy,
opinions,
and attitude,
do little to disrupt
your calm reservoir within.

✦

## MEDITATION

The balance of being open and accepting
to every thought and emotion
that arises in the mind,
while holding on to neither.

# The Calm

Every moment you have two options.

To see everything you have lost,
or to see everything you have gained.
To look at what you can't do,
or to look at what you can do.
To reminisce about the "could have been",
or to live accepting everything that has been.
To see your life as unfair,
or to see your problems in perspective.
To sit in all the suffering,
or see it as an opportunity for growth.
To question everything that is happening to you,
or to trust everything will fall into place.
To feel sad for everything
this moment has taken away from you,
or to feel grateful for all the things
this moment has given you.

Some day's it will feel harder to choose the latter,
and some day's it will seem almost impossible.
But the choice is always there,
you just have to decide each moment
which one you're going to choose.

# Within These Four Walls

ALWAYS STAY FOCUSED ON WHAT YOU DO HAVE

Rolling into another month of the year,
and the visibility of the days passing
are making themselves all too noticeable.
While the absence of
energy,
improvement,
and physical healing,
are making themselves all too invisible.
How many days need to go by until those three things
decide to make themselves seen?
If it's time they need,
I have plenty.
If it's patience they need,
I will persevere.
If it's hope they need,
I'll keep my stores fully stocked.
But if it's reason they need,
I have little.
I have only
trust,
hope,
acceptance,
gratitude,
calm,
and light.
But it's more than some people have,
so I'll hold these things
close to my heart.

## The Calm

And I'll make sure that
even if those other three things decide
it still isn't the time for them to show up,
I'll never give up any of the good things.
I have more than some,
and I have more than I did,
and for now,
that has to be enough.

# Within These Four Walls

## ACKNOWLEDGE IT

Your pain
can't teach you anything
if you always turn away
from its existence.

✦

## NO MUD, NO LOTUS

Without pain,
there could be no growth.
Therefore I honour my pain
for giving me the
ability to grow.

✦

## STAY HERE

When you want to escape suffering,
do not look to the past or the future.
For although your pain lives in the present,
so does peace and happiness.

# The Calm

As human beings, we are always looking for ways to solve our problems and want to know the easiest way to overcome things. So when you are faced with a problem that you can't easily solve, like M.E or Chronic Lyme, you have to suddenly change your whole philosophy as to what you've been taught all your life. You have to accept there is no easy way around it. You have to accept there is no quick fix. You have to surrender to the fact that healing will not happen overnight. And all of this is so much easier said than done.

It's no wonder so many people resist in these moments as a small part of us might still believe there must be a simple way to get around it all, as this is how we've lived our whole life up to this point. But the bravest and most courageous thing you can do is to say, "I accept how things are, I accept there is little I can do to change them, but I also accept that this won't be forever". Because when you do this, and finally let go of that resistance and surrender to the moment, something so beautiful happens. You discover that even amidst all the chaos, you can still be happy and at peace.

# Within These Four Walls

One virus was all it took to change my life. One virus was all it took to flip the path I thought I had planned and to shove me on a completely different, unknown path. One virus was all it took to see my health slowly slip out of my hands until barely visible grains were left. One virus is all it can take to snatch the word 'me' from your vocabulary and slip a dot into the middle of the word to create M.E and consequently, change your world entirely.

And it can, and does, happen to anyone. School children, teenagers, students, adults, parents. A whole population of people silently selected to never recover from viruses so many will get. But what are you left with at the end of that? A population of people who can join together like no other. A population of people all connecting through a single thread. Our voices come together like droplets of water seeking each other out, and standing side by side, we form a tsunami of love and support. A community built like no other.

I know one day our collective voice will be heard, and we will finally get the awareness, treatment, and cure so so desperately needed. And I know it won't be the result of one single voice, but the result of an army of voices, standing together in unity, simply asking to be heard.

# The Calm

PEACE IS EVERYWHERE

There will be times
when things work out for you,
and there will be times
when things don't.
There will be times
when you love where you are,
and there will be times
when you can't wait to get away from here.

But know this:
whatever is happening to you,
wherever you are,
however you feel about it,
there is always peace
to be unearthed
and a life
to be lived,
waiting here
for you.

## THE ART OF WRITING

She wants to still her mind
so she opens her heart
and lets the words flood out,
spilling across the page
like the words needing to be written
may soon be forgotten.
But once they are seen
their power begins to cease,
for the words visible to the eye
do not have the same control
as the ones that live in the mind.
So more and more dance across the page
until the sadness begins to fade
and a calmness takes its place.
For looking at the words upon the paper,
it becomes clear that they are just thoughts,
and nothing more.
And once on the page
they can be released from the mind.
And now the mind is free
to be as still and calm as water,
because once again she is reminded
that thoughts are just that,
thoughts,
not reality.

# The Calm

### GO SLOWLY

Take your time
nurturing your happiness.
This is something you want
for the rest of your life.
Do not rush the process.
Delve deep and plant the goodness.

✦

### REMEMBER

Small acts of kindness
can make someone's day.

✦

### THEY WILL ALWAYS BE THERE

Worries are like dark clouds
you see overhead in the distance;
in that moment, it is not whether it is
going to rain in the future that matters –
it is whether you choose to sit around
waiting for the rain to come.

THIS MOMENT IS A GIFT

The only thing I want to do is to live life deeply in the here and now.

To let go of any expectations or plans and simply let things be what they will be.

To focus on slowing down and taking the time to notice the little things.

To pause when I have my morning cup of tea.

To watch the sun set each evening and take in all the array of colours it produces.

To always embrace the love and joy that's surrounding me.

To prioritise self-care and cuddling loved ones.

To put my phone down and stay attentive on what is happening in this moment.

To listen deeply, talk mindfully, and laugh loudly.

To take deep breaths when things get too much.

To stop worrying about the future or the things that could have been and instead, staying focused on the present and pressing pause on all the magical moments.

# The Calm

I LIVE FOR THESE MOMENTS

There are these moments of happiness
that seize us so tightly we cannot help
but smile at the world around us as we feel
heavy with love and gratitude for this life.
It is in these beautiful moments we think,
"You know what? Life's pretty great."
And if anyone were to ask us,
"If you could be anywhere
in the world right now,
where would you choose to be?"
We would look around,
smile, and answer,
"Right here."

## THE DEPTHS OF HAPPINESS FROM WITHIN

Every time I think I know what true happiness feels like, I find myself falling deeper into it and unearthing even more knowledge and truth. Because that is the thing with happiness, there is no limit as to how far into its depths you can go. It is like a bottomless pit; each time you think you've reached the floor, you discover there are still oceans of room to expand and temples of knowledge yet to be gained.

It's sad to think how many of us spend our lives only knowing the surface, but it is also wonderful to know that this vastness that lives within is always there, whether you decide to explore it or not. Every one of us has oceans of happiness inside of ourselves that can reach depths we've never dreamed of. And it will always be there, waiting for you to delve within and discover it. So be brave and turn your attention inwards, and explore the universe inside of you.

# The Calm

EMBRACING INDIVIDUALITY

I love the fact you will never meet the same two people in life. I love the fact we're literally all one of a kind. I love the fact everyone is their own unique self, and there will be no one else exactly like you on the planet.

But it's so easy to want to be more like someone else, to want to be less "you". You might shy away from your true personality thinking maybe you're too different or a little bit weird. But who you are is already amazing. You don't need to try to change it, you don't need to make excuses for who you are.

So many of us say things like "I'm sorry I'm really..." or "I wish I weren't so..." Don't be afraid that people won't love you for who you are, because they will. If you pretend to be someone you're not, you won't ever get to find your tribe or real friends in life.

You're you, and you are the only you. No one can replace you. No one else can be you as well as you can. Because who you are is solely yours. Embrace it.

GO YOUR OWN WAY

If you are made to stand
in another's shadow
do not think
you have to take two paces forward,
or one pace back,
to reclaim the light.
Instead,
take a step to the side,
go your own way
and create your own spotlight.

# The Calm

FOLLOWING THE CROWD

It's so easy to walk down a path that is not meant for you, simply because everyone else is walking down that path too. But you can feel something isn't right. Maybe it's a feeling of uneasiness. Maybe you feel lost. Maybe it's the feeling of trying to convince yourself too hard that this is the right path for you.

But then you see someone walking down a path completely different from everyone else, and there's something about them that attracts you. Maybe it's the way they seem so free. Maybe it's how at ease and happy they are. Maybe it's their carelessness and go with the flow attitude.

Their courage to walk in the wilderness alone inspires you; it moves you to think maybe you can do the same. Maybe you too can move out of this path that is not for you, and into the wilderness to find your own way.

It is so scary to walk out of the familiar and conventional. But once you've taken that step, know that the hardest part is over. You have acknowledged that the path you were walking on was never meant for you. And although people may question what you are doing, you'll know you've done the right thing, because the weight of trying to fit in, trying to do something because everyone else is, will lift. And it'll be so freeing.

You'll have all this newfound space to explore and work out who you are now – the real you. You are free to go anywhere you want. You are finally free to be you and to go down the path that was meant for you.

# The Calm

LIQUID SUNSHINE

If you are someone who wishes
to grow,
to learn,
to be free,
then you need to surround yourself
with others who seek the same things.
You'll only outgrow everyone else
and find yourself shrinking to be with them.

So stay close to those who make
you feel like liquid sunshine;
warm, open and at ease,
whilst at the same time,
radiant and luminous,
always wanting to shine
that bit brighter.

SELF-BELIEF

Imagine what we could achieve if we all had a little more self-belief and the courage to take that first step. Imagine if we didn't worry over what other people thought about our decisions, and we only worried about what we thought of ourselves. Imagine if we lived our lives not through our failures and successes but through the number of times we gave things a go.

The thing holding us back from taking that first step is so often ourselves. Our fear of failure. Our lack of self-belief. Our uncertainty of the unknown. But maybe we should fear all the chances we didn't take, all the opportunities we said no to instead of yes. You don't often regret trying something, even if it doesn't work out, because you learn from these opportunities. But you do often regret the chances you didn't take.

So have more courage to take those chances that come to you in life because you simply can't know if you're good at something or if you will enjoy it until you try it. Hold more love for yourself to know that if it doesn't work out, you are not defined by your failures. Have more belief in yourself to take that first step.

# The Calm

CHANGE

Change can be so scary and yet it can also be so exciting. Change is where the growth happens, the transformations take place, and the possibilities are endless.

But instead of accepting the changes that come our way, a lot of us stay behind and get stuck. We become overwhelmed with fear as we start to overthink what this change means and how it will affect our future. But we don't have to think about the change. We don't have to label it as good or bad. We don't have to analyse it. We don't have to mentally work out what went wrong or right. We can, instead, just flow with the change. To never overthink it. To just adapt to what is happening.

It is what it is, and maybe we should try and be okay with whatever that is. Embrace the fear and excitement that comes with the change together; be curious about where this change could lead you and try not to hold on to the old this or the old you.

Change can be beautiful, but you have to give it a chance; take a deep breath, step into the change, and allow yourself to see where it will take you.

ACCEPTANCE

You are so brave to accept what you cannot control. What courage you have to realise it is better to let go of those things you can do nothing about than to sit and try and change something that cannot be changed.

It can be so hard though, can't it? To let go of those things you cannot control, because letting go can so often feel like giving up. It can feel like you're saying you like how things are, that you don't mind if they don't change. But acceptance is none of those things. Acceptance is not giving up, because giving up is easy, acceptance is not. It is one of the hardest things to do.

Acceptance is about knowing although you can't change things right now, that doesn't mean time won't change them. It's seeing this moment as not forever, but temporary; a chapter in your story that will one day move on to the next one. It is recognising you have no control over how quickly the next chapter comes, or how long this one will be. But realising it will pass, and for now, you may as well use your energy towards finding peace and happiness in this moment rather than wasting it on trying to change what you have no control over.

You should be so proud for realising this. You should be so proud of how you are seeing your situation. Know you are doing the best thing for yourself by accepting. And if anyone asks you if acceptance is about giving up, you can tell them: acceptance is not about giving up. Acceptance, in fact, requires the highest level of courage; the courage to let go of what you cannot control.

MOTIVATOR

Sometimes you need a day
to stop trying to see the
positives in everything,
to wallow in the sadness,
to feel sorry for yourself,
to give up the hope and trust
that everything is going to be okay,
and to let go of the belief that
you are growing from this.

Because the sadness
you feel from this day
will remind you
exactly why
you try your best to
stay positive
in the first place.

# The Calm

UNEARTHING PEACE

You do not need to have everything together or under control to feel peaceful. You do not need to wait until your external circumstances are calm, as no place you find yourself in will ever be free from noise. Because whatever path you are on, there is always peace to be discovered.

There is peace within the broken pieces, shining in through the cracks. There is peace in the unknown, following you through the wilderness. There is peace in the mess, tumbling out in unexpected places. There is peace in the chaos, sitting silently in the middle.

There is peace in the little things: the deep breaths, nature, staying present, slowing down, taking everything one moment at a time. And there is peace in the letting in: the letting in of calm, gratitude, contentment, and quietude.

There is peace in the release: releasing hurt caused by others, negative habits weighing you down, relationships bringing about stress. And there is peace in the letting go: the letting go of worry, fear, resistance, and doubt, replacing these things with trust, hope, compassion, and acceptance. Letting go of what could have been and what might still come.

Peace comes from both allowing in the things that invoke peace within you whilst letting go of everything taking your peace away from you – and knowing that wherever you are, there is always peace to be unearthed.

# The Calm

TWENTY-FOUR HOURS

Tomorrow is not another day.
Tomorrow is a new day.
It is a chance to make new memories, new experiences, new moments.
It's a day you have never seen before and will never see again.
It cannot be exchanged, replaced, or refunded.
You have been given these twenty-four hours to use as you will.
You can waste them or use them for good.
Tomorrow can be filled with joyful, happy moments.
But it is up to you to fill it with these moments.
Remember you can turn over a new leaf every hour if you choose.
Every day is the chance to learn something new, so handle it with care.
You have lived your whole life up to this moment, to come to this day.
Make the most of it.
Tomorrow is yours.

THINGS I KNOW TO BE TRUE

Those people who make you question yourself – don't let their words faze you. Life's too short to stop every time someone questions you. Keep going.

You do not like every person you meet in life, therefore, not every person who meets you will like you. So don't let it disconcert you too much if you're not someone's cup of tea, it's often nothing to do with you.

Criticism from others is inevitable – the choice to listen to it though is yours.

Not everyone will understand your path or the life you choose to live. That's okay. Don't waste your energy trying to explain or justify it to them. Let them go and carry on down your path and don't look back.

Everyone is entitled to their own opinions.

The people most likely to question the choices you make are probably the ones who understand you the least.

# The Calm

BECOME A BETTER YOU

Stop expecting
more from others,
and start expecting
more from yourself.

Focus less on how
they should be reacting,
and start focusing more
on how you wish to react.

Sit and reflect on your
actions with honesty
and non-judgement.

Take the time to understand
and learn how you can
grow and improve.

Ask yourself:
Am I living up to the person I want to be?
Am I living as my best self?

Lead your life by example,
not by opinion.

GOOD AND BAD PEOPLE

"Why do good people suffer?" she asked.

"What makes you good," Wisdom replied, "and some people bad? For if you are saying good people don't deserve to suffer, then you are suggesting bad people do deserve to suffer. But what you are forgetting is that those you hold in your mind as bad people have likely already gone through so much suffering. So why should you be allowed to avoid suffering and those who have already suffered, be made to suffer more?"

# The Calm

TRUE COMPASSION

Compassion
is not about feeling sorry for someone,
or feeling pity for them,
or seeing them lesser than yourself.
True compassion,
is about seeing the world
through their eyes.
Recognising,
you are one and the same,
and that
you could just have
easily been them,
and they could just
have easily been you.

# Within These Four Walls

START FROM WITHIN

She asked the universe,
"In a world full of so much suffering and pain,
how can I make the world a better place?"

The universe replied,
"How can you expect the world to be a more peaceful
place if you do not first create peace within you?

For if you are happy,
there is one less sad person in the world.
If you are positive,
there is one less negative person in the world.
If you love all beings,
there is one less person hating in the world.
If you are satisfied,
there is one less greedy person in the world.
If you are kind,
there is one less violent person in the world.
If you are at peace,
there is one less angry person in the world.

Change the worlds within you
and you will change the world around you."

# The Calm

- You have come further this year than you realise.
- There are no deadlines in life, you don't have to have completed anything by a certain age or year. There are only the deadlines you set for yourself, but these can be changed and adapted.
- Let go of the habits that are weighing you down or adding negativity to your life. You really don't need them.
- Recognise your true priorities in life and always put them first above everything else. The other things can always be done tomorrow, or the day after, or the day after that.
- There are still 180 days left this year. So much can happen in one day, let alone 180 of them, so have hope that things could still change a whole lot more for you.
- Do what you need to do each day in order to heal and grow: create those pockets of calm and carve out time and space for yourself.
- To get to where you want to be, you can only focus and work on who you are today.
- Breathe. There is still so much more from this year to come.

# Within These Four Walls

GRANTED

Do not take life for granted because
you do not know what will happen in the future,
let alone what will happen in the next five minutes.
You could become so ill with fatigue
you can't leave the house for years.
You could be involved in a car accident and
never know what it means to feel your legs again.
You could have loved ones taken
away from you too young.
Do not assume
that because you have these things now,
they will always be there,
for they are being taken away from
someone in the world every second.
The ability to leave the house...gone.
The ability to walk...gone.
The ability to say "I love you" to someone...gone.
All of these are possible,
for the first person is me,
and the others are my friends.
So appreciate what you have,
before time makes you appreciate what you had.

# The Calm

Those moments
that the earth produces
a sight so beautiful,
it is truly breath-taking.
You cannot believe
you have never noticed
how incredibly beautiful
the world is
before this moment.
But the earth
is already filled
with so much
beauty,
wonder,
and life.
It was not the earth
that had just decided
to be beautiful,
it was you deciding
to show up for this moment
to witness it.

# Within These Four Walls

## LOOK OUTSIDE

You don't always need to travel
the world to see beauty,
sometimes you just need to
look out your window.

❖

## THE POWER OF NATURE

There is nothing more peaceful
than when one stares up at
the clear night sky and see's
the moon shining in all its glory.

❖

## DISCOVERY

When the walls of my
physical world decreased,
I looked within
and found a universe
waiting to be discovered
and explored.

# The Calm

IMAGINATION SAVED ME

My body may be injured, but my mind is still whole and can experience peace. My body may be stuck between these four walls, but my mind is free. It is free to travel all over the world without having to move my feet. It is the passport I so often desperately need. The plane ticket that can take me anywhere I want in an instant.

I can visit places I've been to before. I can go to places entirely imaginary. I can go to places only known in books and films. I can meet new people. I can bring along friends, pets, or family members. I can befriend fictional characters.

I can go on adventures. I can swim in the ocean. I can run along the beach. I can hike up mountains. I can dance under the moonlight. I can watch beautiful sunsets. I can feel the sun on my face and the sand underneath my feet.

I can create safe spaces to visit whenever I need them. I can create worlds to fall into when my own world becomes too much. I can do anything and everything because, in my mind, I know that even the sky isn't the limit.

NEW SEASON

Maybe this new season should be about slowing down; giving yourself more deep breaths and rest. Maybe this season should be about creating more space; more time for yourself and more time for healing. Maybe this season should be about trusting the unknowns; letting go of the fear, doubt, and worry, and being kind to yourself as you brave this new spell.

It's tempting to walk into this new season afraid of what could go wrong; afraid nothing will change once again, afraid of what this new season might bring. But this season could also be the beginning of something new. It could be a time when things finally start to fall into place for you, where you feel hope and trust with every step you take. Or maybe nothing big will happen, but all the little things will add up to something beautiful. Maybe it will be all those in-between moments that make this season special.

Because whatever happened or didn't happen in the previous season, that chapter is now closed. You are here, walking into a brand-new season, full of endless possibilities. Don't let the path behind you trick you into thinking this season will be the same as the last. You are not facing that way anymore: you are looking forward. You are looking out at a horizon of places you have not been. You are looking into the unknown and the equally beautiful.

It may scare you to see all this vastness in front of you, but that's okay. You only need to take this new season one step at a time. Let the horizon remind you of the endless possibilities to come, filling you with hope and trust that things will be okay, and let this moment remind you the only thing that matters right now is this next step forward.

# Within These Four Walls

## MOVE WITH LIFE

Life is like the wind:
you can control neither
the direction or the speed,
and to try and walk against it
will only make life
more difficult.
The only thing you can do
to make it easier
is to move with it
and see where
it will take you.

❖

## THE RECIPE FOR ACCEPTANCE

Letting go of the resistance of wanting things to be
different from what they are.
+
Accepting there is little you can do to change them.
+
Recognising that this isn't forever and everything is
impermanent.
+
A whole lot of courage to do all of the above.

# The Calm

BREATHE

Slow down. Stop. Pause. Connect with your breath, so you and the breath are one. Breathe. Breathe deeply. Breathe until you can feel the breath reaching the very soles of your feet. Feel the air filling up your body with the inhale, and feel it leaving with the exhale. Feel the clarity and calm taking over your mind with every breath. Keep going until this calmness seeps all over and you feel the weight of your body getting heavier with each exhale. You now realise your only thought is this very breath...

Welcome back to the present moment. Doesn't it feel good to be back here? And what wonderful insight you have gained that the breath is the quickest gateway to the present moment. You connect with the breath; you connect with the moment. To breathe is to be present. Keep focusing on the breath and you'll keep being present. Now, remember that this gateway is always here for you whenever you may need it.

END OF THE ROAD

There will be so many times in your life where it will feel like the end of the road. When you fail your exams and think that is the end of your career. When you lose your job, your relationship, your place at school or university, your marriage, or something else that provided you with security for the future. Although in that moment it can feel like everything is falling apart, that you have reached the end of the road, know that this is not the end. It is simply the last page of a chapter, with the next one completely unwritten.

It's understandable why in these moments, with no story ahead of you, no path you can see, no security for the future, it can often feel like the end of the road. But all that has happened is you are being taken on a different route. You are required to find another path, a new way forward. And you will. Why? Because you have had these moments in the past, you have felt it was the end of the road before, and even if it was a different scenario or place in your life, you still got through it. You still found a way forward that brought you to this moment.

And the likelihood is this new path you had to find taught you things you would never have learnt if your last chapter had not ended so abruptly. It took you to places you never knew existed, and you found ways around that you didn't even know were an option or a possibility before this detour.

So know that when a door closes on you, when your path ahead gets blocked, when everything feels like it is falling apart – this is only the beginning. And maybe one day you will be able to look back and see that when that door closed on you, it was the best thing that could have ever happened to you.

Always remember that there is no one path in life, and often, it is only when your planned path up ahead is no longer accessible are you then able to see all the alternative routes out there. So even though in the moment it might feel as though you've lost everything, take heart that the end of the road is really the beginning of something new.

# Within These Four Walls

## STOP WAITING

Greed says,
"Wait until everything has fallen into place,
then you can be happy."

Wisdom says,
"Become happy, and everything
will fall into place."

✦

## MAKE YOUR OWN

"Where did you find that?"
she asked her friend,
"I've been looking for it everywhere!"

Clutching a jar of happiness,
the friend replied,
"I made it myself."

✦

## CONTENTMENT

The concept of contentment is very simple; it's to
believe we already have everything we need in this
moment to be happy.

# The Calm

NOW IS THE BEST TIME TO BE HAPPY

Happiness is not something to wait for. It should not be something you only plan for your future, because you aren't living in the future, you're only living in this moment.

If you always wait for your happiness, putting it off until things fall into place first, then all you are doing is denying yourself the happiness you could be experiencing right here, right now.

Happiness is not a destination to arrive at: it is something to create and practise for this moment. If you're always waiting to be happy, then that's all you'll be doing – waiting. And all this time you've spent waiting could have instead been time spent being happy.

Happiness can only be found in the present moment, so don't wait for your happiness to come to you – meet it here in this moment because now is the best time to be happy.

HOUSEBOUND

You say,
I have not seen the world.
I say,
I have seen the depths of the world within myself.

You say,
I have not lived.
I say,
I have already lived a hundred lives.

You say,
I have not seen beauty.
I say,
I have watched a thousand sunsets.

You say,
I have so much more to gain.
I say,
I have everything I need.

You say,
I have a life waiting for me.
I say,
I have my life right here.

MOVING ON

As I've been stuck here in this house, I'm aware everyone else has been moving on. Moving on to new friends, new partners, new cities, new jobs. They've started and finished university degrees. They've begun and ended relationships. They've travelled to foreign countries and settled in new homes. They've got new friendship groups and new jobs.

I know that when I leave this house, it'll be a shock for me to realise just how much everything has changed and how everyone I once knew has moved on and grown up.

But in so many ways, I too have moved on. I've moved on from wasting my energy on things that hold little value to me. I've moved on from focusing on others to concentrating on myself. I've moved on from searching for romantic love to finding peace and happiness in my own company. I've moved on from worrying about what others think to doing what always feels best for me. I've moved on from seeking approval and achievements to seeking growth and inner peace.

I am not the same person who walked into this house for the last time all those years ago. I have moved on and grown up too, I just can't put my kind of growth on paper, and I'm so grateful for that. Because this is my path – it has given me so much more than it has ever taken away, and I wouldn't have it any other way.

Let's stay in touch!

**Follow me on social media:**

**Instagram:** @mindfullyevie
(https://www.instagram.com/mindfullyevie/)
**Facebook:** @mindfullyevie
(https://www.facebook.com/mindfullyevie/)
**Pinterest:** Mindfully Evie
(https://www.pinterest.co.uk/mindfullyevie/)
**Goodreads:** Mindfully Evie
(https://www.goodreads.com/mindfullyevie)

**My blog:** www.mindfullyevie.com

**For all enquires:** evie@mindfullyevie.com

Please note that 10% of all profits from the book sales will go to charity, split equally between 'Invest in M.E' and 'Lyme Disease Action'. To find out more about these charities, visit:
http://www.investinme.org/
https://www.lymediseaseaction.org.uk

xx